Practical Tools for

Reinventing the Dying Church

Tom Cheyney

General Editor

Copyright © 2017 Renovate Publishing Group, Orlando Florida. Tom Cheyney Et. Al.
All rights reserved.
ISBN: 978-0-9987384-5-1
ISBN-10: 0-9987384-5-X

The Renovate Quarterly

Tools such as this are generously provided through the investment of partners and donors for the purpose of raising up viable tools by and for those working in the field of church revitaliztion and renewal.Each gift to the Renovate Group helps equip church revitalizers with practical resources for turning around their church. In an effort to save our nation, the Renovate National Church Revitalization Conference trains and prepares pastors, laity, and denominational leaders for the work of church revitalization and renewal.

To partner with and donate to the cause of revitalizing churches all across North America you many donate at: www.renovateconference.org/donate.

For any gift of $500 or more, you will receive the seven book set of Renovate Resources published by the Renovate Publishing Group. All donations to support the cause of church revitalization and renewal are tax deductible.

TABLE OF CONTENTS

Chapter One (12)
Maintaining Relevance for Church Revitalization and Renewal
By Tom Cheyney

Chapter Two (23)
Lessons for the First Time Revitalizer
By Rodney Harrison

Chapter Three (26)
Know Your Audience to Maximize Church Revitalization
By Joel R. Breidenbaugh

Chapter Four (29)
Regaining Relevance for Revitalization
By Mark Weible

Chapter Five (32)
Where Does Church Revitalization Begin?
By Jim Grant

Chapter Six (35)
Survival Tips for a Young Pastor
By Rob Arnold

Chapter Seven (37)
Relevant Preaching and the Revitalization of the Church
By Paul E. Smith

Chapter Eight (40)
"Danger, Will Robinson!": Dangerous Threats to the Church Revitalization Movement
By Terry Rials

Chapter Nine (43)
Successful Student Pastors Have Well Defined Expectations

By Drew Cheyney

Chapter Ten (47)
Reimagining Your Children's Ministry Volunteers for Renewal
By Bill Hegedus

Chapter Eleven (50)
A Change of Heart:
The Role of Prayer in the Revitalization of the Church
By Chris Irving

Chapter Twelve (53)
The Pastor's Personal Life and Leadership Capacity
By Greg Kappas

Chapter Thirteen (56)
Desire for Authenticity Not Cultural Relevancy
By Jim Grant

Chapter Fourteen (58)
The Greatest Challenge in Revitalization
By John Kimball

Chapter Fifteen (60)
Tribal Leadership and Church Revitalization
By Kenneth Priest

Chapter Sixteen (64)
Running with Tortoises
By Rob Hurtgen

Chapter Seventeen (67)
Pitfalls of Revitalizers
By Michael Atherton

Chapter Eighteen (71)
Getting to Know Your Congregation
By Tracy W. Jagger

Chapter Nineteen (76)
Your Best Church Year
How to Have a Breakthrough Year
Ron Smith

Conclusion (83)
Elements Most Critical for a Church to Turnaround
By Tom Cheyney

Appendix One (85)
Key Church Revitalization and Renewal Definitions
By Tom Cheyney

Appendix Two (97)
Suggested Church Revitalization Bibliography
By Tom Cheyney

Acknowledgements

It has been a pleasure to watch students grow to such a level that they move from being doctoral students to fellow soldiers in the cause of revitalizing churches all across North America. These men who have partnered with me and the Renovate National Church Revitalization Conference and are found within this compilation have proven themselves as worthy church revitalizers and turn around pastors. All of these leaders have been accomplished students within the field of revitalization and have now become tremendous church revitalizers and practioners for this cause of church revitalization. In a day where many are becoming interested in saving a rapidly declining church, it is a joy to see these leaders becoming the truly qualified voices in the work.

Recently, an individual who knew of the work we have done with the RENOVATE National Church Revitalization Conference and the supportive resources such as The Church Revitalizer Magazine, suggested that I write a series of small chapters on various tools that could save a dying church. As a result of our conversation, *Practical Tools for Reinventing the Dying Church* was birthed, and the men who ultimately contributed to this collection of chapters immediately came to mind. Their willingness to join the cause yet again is so refreshing, and thus began our journey towards creating this tool for churches of all sizes in need of church revitalization and renewal.

Practical Tools for Reinventing the Dying Church

Each year while working with churches both locally where I live in central Florida and where all of these men minister, we have been blessed to have a national multi denominational platform through the RENOVATE National Church Revitalization Conference to continue to raise up the topic of church revitalization and renewal. While there are many out there in various institutions who are brushing off their concepts from the 1970's, let's be quick to say that there is no magic pill for church revitalization and renewal; what works in one setting may not work in another. God desires to create a unique you.

I am blessed each day to serve the Greater Orlando Baptist Association (GOBA). This network of churches is changing the way we have done associational work across the Southern Baptist denomination. No longer bound by geography, GOBA has raised the bar by working with churches, networks, and partners to plant healthy churches, to revitalize those churches in need of renewal, and to develop leaders equipped for the ministry through the GOAL Leadership Development Training. The Renovate National Church Revitalization Conference is one of many new things that have impacted Christianity cross-denominationally. To the wonderful pastors and laity who have partnered with us in these endeavors for the work of the Lord, may I say thank you.

To the many committed church revitalization practitioners who join with me annually to make the Renovate National Church Revitalization Conference the largest conference focused on helping declining churches, I say thank you to you as well. Your gifts and your godly compassion for hurting churches make my heart leap. And to those just beginning the journey: seek God's best and become the best you can be in and through Him daily so that you can become a vessel fully developed for the work of a Church Revitalizer.

One particular behind-the-scenes individual who carries a large responsibility within the entire Renovate Group and all that we do in church revitalization and renewal is Gerald Brown. Gerald is an incredible pastor of a growing church and former church plant. If you enjoy anything we do through Renovate Resources, you can be sure that he is the one leading us to excellence. Appreciation and admiration go out to this godly pastor who directs us in all design aspects for the work we do. Thank you, Gerald, for your hard work and constant commitment to keep the cause of revitalization before the churches across North America.

Lastly to my Strategic Director of the Renovate Conference and the Renovate Group, Mark Weible, I say thank you for knowing and showing daily how to do team. You have lightened my load many times so I could find an afternoon or evening to finish some of this work. Your wisdom and

Practical Tools for Reinventing the Dying Church

commitment to the cause of planting and revitalizing churches is such a gift. Though many will never know you around the nation, they are blessed everyday by your hard work and call to help new and hurting pastors. Mark, you quietly influence thousands of Church Revitalizers monthly by the work you do to advance the cause of church revitalization and renewal. The best is yet to come. – Tom Cheyney

CHAPTER ONE
Maintaining Relevance for Church Revitalization and Renewal
By Tom Cheyney

Relevance is a big topic these days when it comes to the rapidly declining church and what can be done about the plateau or decline. Would you classify the particular church you have been called to lead as appropriately relevant any longer? In this article, I would like for us to reflect upon the idea of the local church's relevance in the community it serves. Relevance is certainly one of the chief obstacles for most congregations fighting the throws of rapid decline.

Recently, a staff member told me of a conversation they had with a church that was in rapid decline. What they wanted from our organization was not the assistance we had already been providing for the last four years, but now something more. They asked for us to fund a particular staff member to come to their church and do the things that they no longer wanted to do. What they were coming to realize was the five specific options they had for consideration four years ago were no longer viable, since they had chosen to sit down and do nothing but complain about the present church revitalizer and why both he as well as our organization expected them to work at bringing the church out of its decline. The last words that came from their lips were that the only thing we wanted was their building. It is often through revitalization efforts that it becomes obvious that a church has waited too long to do something, it is usually when they see the writing on the wall that closure is imminent that they then want help. I have said it publicly and will say it over and over again that if a church waits too long to begin the church revitalization journey, many times the only thing any church revitalization group can do is to close the present church, deed the property over to a church revitalization network such as an association, and allow them to put either a church planter or church revitalizer in place in an attempt to keep a gospel lighthouse at that specific location. The church that is working towards revitalization and renewal needs to reply to the needs of the world in an applicable way, while caring out its Biblical directive to continue to make disciples if it is going to remain relevant. Jesus modeled relevance for us. He met people right where they were in His culture. He powerfully ministered in the middle of the diverse social spectrum that surrounded Him (Jews, Gentiles, Pharisees, Samaritans, and Romans) and He contextualized the message in a way His culture could relate.

Random House Dictionary has defined relevance as: the condition of being relevant, or connected with the matter at hand.[1]

With the world changing and the local church slow to respond to such changes, maintaining relevance is critical in this post-post-modern age. Someone has humorously alleged, "There are four signs of approaching age: baldness, bifocals, bridges, and bulges!" We are changing each and every day. A church is a living organism made up of spiritual believers who have had a salvation experience with our Lord Jesus Christ. As such we have made a commitment to the responsibility of carrying out the commands of our Lord. History seems to dictate that prior "movements" became "monuments" when they failed to discern the times in "becoming all things to all men so that by all possible means some might be saved". The greater question is: Are we open to preaching the gospel "by all possible means"? If the answer is "yes" then it's time to get relevant. If the answer is

---

[1] Relevance. Dictionary.com Unabridged. Random House, Inc. http://dictionary.reference.com/browse/relevance (accessed: July 08, 2015).

"no", then its only a matter of time before our movement resembles a monument as did many other great movements before us. Relevance is the relational key in keeping our timeless message truly timeless. The New Testament church is a spiritual, a functioning, a relational, and a reproducing body. Let's look at the positive side of churches that are being revitalized and how they are working to keep their relevance as they relate to the communities they serve.

R – Relational

We live in a world where people need relationships that are cultivated and sustained. The church is a social, relational organization. A relevant church needs structures to assist in developing and strengthening relationships. A relevant church seeks to create community. Churches that fail to start new groups and relevant groups have decided to die. Relationship building will either make you or break you as a pastor/leader. If you are effective in drawing people around you into lasting relationships, you will have a greater chance to be effective. What makes a church secure and stable is not mere friendliness, but true concern, compassion, and caring for others. Most declining churches give little thought to how relationships develop within the church. There needs to be a purposeful commitment to relationship building with other believers (most of this is outside of small groups)! I have asked hundreds of unchurched people the question, "What is the one thing you would look for in a church?" That simple research indicates that more than anything else, people want to build meaningful relationships. As Christians, we know that people ultimately are looking for relationships with God. In today's world, if the church is going to reach the unchurched, it must build bridges of relationships.

Practical Tools for Reinventing the Dying Church

E – Evangelism

Declining churches often replace evangelism with feel-good inward focused events, which can appeal to the already initiated individual of the church, does little to draw or compel new people to the church. Relevant churches keep practices of effective evangelism front and center. Declining churches create events which provide a good time for the present membership, but does little to reach a lost community. In order to remain relevant, the declining church needs a process to identify, cultivate and track prospects. They need to pray for lost people and keep the subject of lost people before the membership. The revitalizing church must have a plan to mobilize members for the task of evangelism. An ongoing plan to train members in evangelism is critical if a dying church wants to see a turnaround. The church revitalizer must model evangelism and apprentice those who could assist in the evangelization of the community around the church. We have learned that revival and renewal occurs when the Holy Spirit makes inroads into the souls of the least likely and the disenchanted. So, we need to start praying and be prepared for the Spirit of God to move us outside the box. Any effective evangelism strategy has a plan to deploy the trained members into the field. If a church renewal effort is going to be successful, the church will need an effective plan to follow-up and disciple those who accept Jesus as Savior and Lord. This is one of the key ingredients towards revitalizing a dying church.

L – Loving

Displaying the love of the Lord displays a church's ability to attract and connect with people at a heart level. Showing love is a way for church members to draw people to themselves, not because they are charismatic, but because they care about people and see the best in them. They relate at a heart level and trust comes easy. This is not an issue of whether or not large numbers of people flock to you, but whether people who know you seem to migrate to you or away from you. That's an important question to ask of your church and its membership. When you do hook up with people, do you quickly connect at a heart level?

People like you best when you are yourself. They may not all like you, but they will like you best when you are yourself. They can trust you when they know that "what they see is what they get." Be yourself.

E – Evolving

Relevant ministry is the buzzword among many church revitalizers as we work to help the church evolve and stay relevant. Some churches are open to such conversation while others are afraid to think about what their church has become and the steps they must take to allow it to evolve into something much healthier. The world is changing faster than it ever has before, and without sacrificing the Truth of the Gospel, the church needs to change with it. Evolving one's church towards a future that impacts culture and community is important. There are some things pastors and churches can do to make sure they do not miss opportunities to minister to people in the midst of a changing culture. Networking a struggling church with a healthy one that is willing to come alongside and assist is a tremendous way to begin the journey back towards health. These churches can bring value and support to the membership of a declining church and offer encouragement while giving direction. This connecting of healthy churches with dying ones helps bring fresh vision and ideas back to the community. Keep in mind is that change is not new to the church. Churches have been evolving in different ways, and for different reasons, since the beginning of time. Stop resisting the necessary changes that just might save your church. The apostle Paul was relevant in his culture by becoming a Jew to the Jew, and a Greek to the Greek. Are we willing to sincerely engage our culture with the love and message of Jesus? If so, are we willing to make the adjustments that are necessary? The need to remain relevant applies not just to the pastor, but also to the entire priesthood of believers represented in the local church.

V – Vision

Since the early 1990s, there has been considerable emphasis placed on the visioning process. With that has come a lot of confusion. Ministry leaders often misunderstand the issue of vision. A biblical understanding of vision is an appropriate step for bringing clarity to this issue. Where there is no revelation, the people cast off restraint (Prov. 29:18). It is clear in Acts 16 that the apostle Paul's motivation for going to Macedonia was a compelling vision or revelation that he received from God. In verse 9 we are told that, *"During the night Paul had a vision of a man of Macedonia standing and begging him, 'Come over to Macedonia and help us.'"* Immediately, Paul redirected his actions in response to this vision. As a result, the gospel was preached and the church was established at Philippi. In the same way, church revitalization must flow out of a clear vision from God. Any other motivation, no matter how noble, is not sufficient. Therefore, it is essential that before one begins the journey of church revitalization, that he understand what it means to receive a vision from God. For Paul, the vision he received was so specific and clear that it required a new direction. There was a new sense of authority in Paul's life. He was compelled toward this new vision. God's revelation tells of what He wants to accomplish in the reaching of a certain people group at a particular point in the future as a result of His church being faithfully revitalized. It is important to understand that this kind of vision is not created, for it already exists within the heart of God. Therefore, it is discovered as God reveals it to the listening church revitalizer. This revealed vision must be shared by the church revitalizer and the local body of Christ. Proverbs 29:18 has been interpreted by many as, *"Where there is no vision, the people perish* (KJV)." A descriptive translation describes the verse like this: *"Where there is no revelation, the people cast off restraint* (NKJV)." A personal translation may be, *"When they do not have a word from God, everyone does what is right in his own eyes."* When believers are not hearing from God, there will be spiritual anarchy in the lives of the people of God. Since a fresh vision is the result of hearing from God, it is important that the church revitalizer spend time alone with God in order to hear Him clearly. For those who are initiators by nature, it is important for the visioning process to include time for prayer and fasting. A vision from God will become clearer and more intense over time.

There are countless ways to communicate vision, but the communication of the vision must be intentional. Therefore, the role of the vision caster is a primary one for the church revitalizer. He will need to constantly cast the vision throughout the process of revitalization and renewal.

A – Adapting

In Genesis 12:1-4 God gave Abram a revelation of what He wanted to accomplish in and through him. *"The Lord had said to Abram, 'Leave your country, your people and your father's household and go to the land I will show you. I will make you into a great nation and I will bless you; I will make your name great, and you will be a blessing. I will bless those who bless you, and whoever curses you I will curse; and all peoples on earth will be blessed through you.' So Abram left, as the Lord had told him; and Lot went with him. Abram was seventy-five years old when he set out from Haran."* Notice Abram's response to God's revelation. Abram adapted immediately, and left to do what the Lord revealed to him. A good question to consider is, "If God revealed a new thing to you as the church revitalizer in regards to what He wants to accomplish in and through you, how long would it take you and your church to get in a position to respond?" Being prepared for the task of revitalization is about spiritually positioning ourselves to respond to God's activity around us.

Regardless of the model you use for one's revitalization effort being able to adapt will allow you many opportunities to reach a new milepost and move towards significant renewal. Every church revitalizer should have a ministry to the body and a mission to the world. When this is happening, a new milepost is being accomplished. This signifies that the renewing church has reached a new level of healthy maturity and another milepost has been realized. While mileposts may vary, each milepost serves as a key organizing principle for accomplishing the vision received from God. Mile posting allows us to ensure that healthy systems are in place prior to initiating the revitalization process. When there is a conflict between the calendar and the completion of a milepost, the calendar should be adjusted. Churches that are adapting themselves to receive our diversifying culture will be churches that thrive in the next ten years. Begin noticing the demographics of the broader community around you, and find ways to welcome them in your building. Adapt and embrace the changes that are right for your community as you

Practical Tools for Reinventing the Dying Church

move forward to bring the Kingdom of Heaven to earth. We ought to be discerning and creative enough to find fresh ways of pointing people to the Redeemer in a way that the least likely will start coming into the Kingdom. An adaptable church is only possible when an adapting pastor leads it. Adapt or die, it is your choice. Chose to become adaptable.

N – No Excuses

It was Benjamin Franklin who said, "He that is good for making excuses is seldom good for anything else." We are skillful at the art of making excuses, aren't we? "I don't know how." "I didn't understand." "I couldn't find the right tools." "The voices told me to clean all the guns today." "I threw out my back bowling." "I have a doctor's appointment." Do you ever catch yourself making excuses when things don't turn out as you had expected in your church? Have you ever tried to explain away why you didn't, couldn't, shouldn't or simply wouldn't do something? If so as a church revitalizer, these are subtle signs that indicate you are living a life of excuses, which prevent you from reaching your full potential for revitalization and renewal.

Declining or dying churches and church leaders often make various excuses for why they are not revitalizing their church. Some fear the failure around them and they make an excuse. Others are embarrassed because of what they thought would happen in their church has not. Some fear the things they must do to bring about the change needed for renewal so they make excuses. Still others lack confidence in their ability to revitalize the church. To eliminate excuses from our lives we must first look at eliminating all traces of fear. Fear traps and locks us away within our comfort zone. Living a life of excuses can have very serious and lasting consequences. Not only will excuses prevent you from reaching your full potential, but they will also hold you back from recognizing opportunities, talents and skills you might have to help you overcome your problems. If you don't challenge yourself to reach new heights, you will never really know what you're capable of. New opportunities lie hidden around every corner; however, you will never find them if you riddle your mind with constantly finding reasons to make excuses. Here are some of the most used excuses for why one has not revitalized their church:

The task is demanding.
My talent is inadequate.
The time is not right.
The teaching is dangerous.
I cannot change.

In the Christian world, we can find all sorts of excuses not to obey God's voice: "It's the preacher's job." "It's not my gift." "I've already served, let someone else do it." "I'm too busy or too tired or too old or too young." It has been said, "Excuses are tools of the incompetent, and those who specialize in them seldom go far." Gabriel Meurier stated, "He who excuses himself, accuses himself." Jeremiah had every excuse ready when God called him to be a prophet. His excuses are often our excuses for not heeding God's voice when he calls. Countering each excuse was a promise from God.

C – Courageous

Church revitalizers need to be willing to take risks for the good of the local church they serve. They need to be strong and of courage. In Joshua Chapter One, God instructs Joshua three times to *"be strong, and be courageous"*. Such easy instructions, but how is he to be strong, and courageous? It's easy sometimes to be cocky, and pretend to be brave, but what Joshua needed was true bravery and courage.

God not only directs Joshua to be "strong, and courageous," but he dictates to him how to be so. To live the kind of life that God wants us to in the society where we live, we too need courage the same way that Joshua did. Sometimes it's hard to be strong and courageous. God says we are to stand on His promises. If we are to accomplish what God calls us and instructs us to do, we as well must stand on the promises. The problem is many churches in need of revitalization are sitting on the premises instead of standing on the promises. Additionally, we can sense God's presence. How can Joshua lead with confidence, how can he confront the battles that lie ahead? He can because the same God that was with Moses is with him. We have a God that will not forsake, and one that will not fail. Next, we must stay the path like Joshua. If Joshua is to be "strong, and courageous" he must stay the path. Like Joshua, we must not turn, not compromise, not become distracted, must not become detoured from what the will of God is. Faithfulness is the key. Lastly, we must start the process of revitalization and renewal. Many in our declining churches have heard the word of God, and sensed his presence and his leading, but are still just sitting. What are you waiting for? Now is the time to get going. There is ground to cover, battles to be won, jobs that are unfinished, so let's "be strong and courageous" and do it! Let us get going.

E – Engaging

Churches and church revitalizers must engage their community in order to survive. Are you currently addressing the needs of your community with the Gospel? What ongoing outreach events are you offering to the area where your church is located? What are the positive impressions your community has towards you and your church? The church needs to do a better job of sharing the Gospel and its relevance. Those who hear the Good News also have a responsibility to receive the news and act upon what they hear, and to follow where the Holy Spirit leads. There are a number of questions that you can ask to help determine the characteristics of your community and work out where your church interests intersect with the needs of the local community:

- What are the socio-economic and demographic characteristics of the area?
- What are the social, economic and environmental challenges or priorities in this neighborhood?
- What is happening in terms of neighborhood improvement?
- What is the backbone of community economic development?
- What employment growth strategies are promoted in the community?

Just as significantly, you will need to give careful thought to the best methods your church could use to engage the diversity of individuals and groups within the community. Consider that the approach to reaching parents of young children will likely be different from your approach to reaching youth in the community. Ask yourself these following questions:

- What languages are spoken within this community? How I can make sure that print and other forms of communication are accessible to as many community members as possible?
- What physical barriers might prevent community members from participating in ministry opportunities and how can I best address these?
- What is the best location for a meeting or event?
- What is the best time of day for a meeting or event?
- What other established organizations within the community can help encourage people to attend?

Wrapping it up!

If church is to be relevant, then we must be willing to do our part to make it relevant. One of the problems we have as Christians is that we expect the church to awaken us, to get us excited about Jesus, and to motivate us to a new way of life. Well the truth is our faith does not work that way. Following Jesus requires us to be active participants in our spiritual growth by taking part in the spiritual disciplines listed above. When we participate in the spiritual disciplines, we begin to see and hear things in a different light. Words we hear on Sunday morning begin to take on new meaning, and before you know it we are excited and see the relevance of Jesus. Jesus never said following Him would be easy; but He did say the rewards would be great. With so many changes taking place in our culture today, is the church keeping pace? In Paul's first letter to the Corinthians he says:

> *Though I am free and belong to no one, I have made myself a slave to everyone, to win as many as possible. To the Jews I became like a Jew, to win the Jews. To those under the law I became like one under the law (though I myself am not under the law), so as to win those under the law. To those not having the law I became like one not having the law (though I am not free from God's law but am under Christ's law), so as to win those not having the law. To the weak I became weak, to win the weak. I have become all things to all people so that by all possible means I might save some. I do all this for the sake of the gospel, that I may share in its blessings* (1 Corinthians 9:19 – 23).

Our message must never change, but our methods must if we desire to reach the culture we have been commissioned to reach. It is a common mistake. Pastors and churches can be trapped by this misunderstanding and never know it. Specifically, that the church must do little more than open its doors on Sunday, and the non-Christian will come. Research over the past two decades undermines this mistaken notion. People are staying away from churches in record numbers. It is time to ask why some churches are no longer vital links to the unconverted and what can be done to change a faltering outreach to the lost. In some cases, Americans are turned off to both the message and messengers of organized religion. To many, the church has appeared narcissistic and self-serving. Leaders often leave behind shattered lives in the wake of their compromised leadership. The church's reputation was dramatically eroded and confidence in church leadership greatly shaken by the scandals of the 1980's. In 1974, nearly one half of the adult population expressed confidence in religious leaders, but that number plummeted to 22 percent by 1989.

The church must consider the serious question of relevance. In the early 1990's, a denomination surveyed a southern city where it wanted to plant a church. The survey centered on a single question: *Why don't you attend church?* Seventy-four percent of those surveyed indicated they felt there was no value in attending church. Thirty-four percent believed the church had no relevance to the way they lived. While the church does not exist to accommodate secular definitions of relevance, we must also face up to the dilemma framed in the lyrics of an old song: "Why spend our time answering questions no one's asking?"

There is a high cost of not understanding a generation, not doing the homework necessary to gain a fair hearing of the gospel. We must understand that it is possible to be culturally relevant, and at the same time biblically sound in our approach to the unchurched. These two ideas are not mutually exclusive. It has been said, "The only person who likes change is a baby with a wet diaper." That might be a bit of an exaggeration, but from my own observation, most people have some hesitancy toward change. Change takes us out of our comfort zone, it doesn't allow us to relax, it doesn't give us the assurance in life we long for.

Even though we are uncomfortable, and should be uncomfortable, with many of the changes in our culture, we must also understand that this is the culture we have been called

Practical Tools for Reinventing the Dying Church

to minister to. This is our world, and God has placed us here for such a time as this. We have been called to bring the gospel of Jesus Christ to the people of this generation. If we are going to do that, and if we are going to do it effectively, we must take Paul's example as our own, and present the message of Christ in a culturally relevant fashion. I believe the church should be culturally relevant while remaining doctrinally pure.

There are things that are always changing. We change as we grow older. Hopefully we also get wiser, more mature, and are able to have better discernment as we age. We change physically. The ethnic make up of our culture is also changing. The Caucasian population is at zero population growth, while the African American, Hispanic, & Asian populations in our country are experiencing double digit expansion. In fact, by 2050 only half of the nation's population will be Caucasian. The concept of multicultural church revitalization will become increasingly significant as our language, customs, values, relationships, and processes are in a state of flux. Unfortunately, the Church has not kept pace with society.

The church has always adapted its ministry and methods to the culture in which they live and serve. While Jesus, the Bible, and Divine Principles will always be with us and do not change, many other things are in a constant state of flux. Worship styles, technology, outreach methods, teaching styles, and much more are always being adapted to reach those who are unchurched, as well as to disciple those who are already Christ followers. Jesus preached from a boat on the Sea of Galilee, creating a natural amphitheater. Today most ministers use a lapel microphone. Paul wrote on papyrus with a quill and ink, this week I used my Mac Book notebook computer to write this newsletter and developed key training for some of our local pastors. The early church studied from the scrolls and parchments, we have dozens of translations bound together in our choice of bindings and colors. Throughout the week, I open my Logos Bible software and search the scriptures and various commentaries in milliseconds. Paul wore a robe while he was preaching. I do not wear such a robe! The church cannot minister to the people of 2017 with methodology designed to reach the people of 1950's.

When I read through the Bible I find verses that tell me about a new song, a new heaven and earth, new wine, new life, new covenant, new creation, new man, and a new command. Our God is a God of change, and He calls the Church to be willing to change with Him. Want a great recipe for being relevant? Here is a practical one:

Become as Authentic as Possible.

Being an authentic church entails knowing who you are at the deepest level. Authenticity is the foundation of relevance because if you do not understand who you are as a church, and where you are coming from, you cannot possibly lead or influence others. You achieve authenticity through a rigorous inventory of your church's strengths and a systematic mapping of the moments in your church life when you have been both highly effective and extremely gratified. Being real in the moment and able to speak courageously will help you share the truth in love.

Become a Life Long Learner

Achieving mastery as a church revitalizer is essential because, if you have no useful skills, you cannot be useful to others. Mastery goes beyond mere competence and skills. It means approaching one's life and relationships as an act of creation, rather than a reaction to people and events. It means approaching lifelong learning with a sense of fun that adds pleasure and energy to the tasks at hand. It means expanding your principles and practices so that they serve a greater purpose. One achieves mastery through a process of continuous improvement of your talents and abilities. Developing mastery requires the ability to put first things first, to take action before it is forced upon you, and to stay mindful while taking action.

Become More Empathetic as the Leader

Empathy is the capacity to recognize and share feelings being experienced by another being. It is the source of compassion, caring for other people, and the desire to help. It means the ability to experience the same emotions that another

Practical Tools for Reinventing the Dying Church

is feeling, without unnecessary judgment. Empathy creates relevance because it creates the deep connection that brings people together.

Take More Action

It is your actions, ultimately, that make you relevant to others. All the authenticity, mastery and empathy in the world remain sterile, until and unless put into motion. It is through action that you change yourself and change the church. Without action, even a great and brilliant mind and soul remains entirely irrelevant.

What is the challenge before us? We must minister to our culture without compromising our message. To meet the challenge of ministering to our culture without compromising our message, we must have a Biblical worldview. A worldview is quite simply the lenses through which we see our world. Whether you realize it or not, we all have a worldview. What we need to do is make sure our worldview is in line with the Bible's. *"There is neither Jew nor Greek, slave nor free, male nor female, for you are all one in Christ Jesus"* Galatians 3:28. If we are going to see people through Jesus' eyes, if we are to have His worldview, we will not base our feelings and attitudes on a person's skin color, their nationality, their language, or their social status. We will love everyone as God's special creation. Not only do we love these people as God's children, we embrace them as equals.

To meet the challenge of ministering to our culture without compromising our message, we must be willing to embrace new methodologies. The Pharisees approached Jesus and wondered why His disciples were not fasting – why they were not keeping the Law. Jesus responded, *"No one sews a patch of un-shrunk cloth on an old garment. If he does, the new piece will pull away from the old, making the tear worse. And no one pours new wine into old wineskins. If he does, the wine will burst the skins, and both the wine and the wineskins will be ruined. No, he pours new wine into new wineskins"* Mark 2:21-22.

These two brief parables of the old garment and old wineskins illustrate the incompatibility of the old system of Jewish law and tradition with the new cloth and new wine of the gospel of Christ. Jesus was always being questioned about the different methods He used. Jesus embraced what was new & effective for ministry. Jesus was the Master of presenting truth in the language of His culture. He used objects, seeds, soil, situational parables, coins, camels, and fig trees – all things that his audiences could readily identify with. And much of the methodology we employ will do the same thing -- whether it be drama, video, art, music, or stories, they will be used to present the gospel in ways that our culture can identify with.

To meet the challenge of ministering to our culture without compromising our message, we must be creative in worship. The Psalmist says: *"Praise the LORD. Sing to the LORD a new song, and his praise in the congregation of the saints"* (Psalms 149:1). John the revelator said: *"And they sang a new song: "You are worthy to take the scroll and to open its seals, because you were slain, and with your blood you purchased men for God from every tribe and language and people and nation"* (Revelation 5:9). God wants His church to sing a new song. He wants us to creatively worship Him in our worship services. This in no way means that we cannot continue praising God with the grand old hymns, but neither does it mean we can shut out the new songs God is calling His people to sing. This is not an either/or situation, it is a both/and situation.

To meet the challenge of ministering to our culture without compromising our message, we must practice the art of becoming. It's important to note that becoming relevant should never compromise the Gospel. No one has the authority to change the good news of Jesus. If relevance is approached in a way that is culturally sensitive, word-based and Spirit-led, it will never compromise the gospel or the power thereof. So our message does not change, but our methods must as we learn to relate a timeless message to a modern culture through a relatable context. This is making the ministry of Jesus manifest in believers. To follow Paul's example is not easy. In fact, it does not come naturally it only comes supernaturally. We can only adapt to, and minister to our culture, when we make an absolute commitment to it, as did Paul. We are not talking about compromising biblical truth, but being flexible in our approach to both evangelism and ministry. Paul says that he was *"free from all men"*; that is, he was not obligated to conform to any man's ideas of opinions. He had been set free in Christ and was obligated only to be conformed to Christ. But Paul surrendered himself, actually made himself a servant to all men. Why? So that he might win more men to Christ. Paul's going along with the opinions and customs of others does not mean he was compromising his convictions or being two-faced. It means that he was getting next to men, gaining their confidence and trust so they would pay attention to his witness for Christ. It is important to note that becoming relevant should never compromise the Gospel. No one has the authority to change the good news of Jesus. If relevance is approached in a way that is culturally sensitive, word-based and Spirit-led, it will never compromise the gospel or the power thereof. So our message does not change, but our methods must as we learn to relate a timeless message to a modern culture through a relatable context. This is making the ministry of Jesus manifest in believers.

1. Paul became as a Jew to the Jews, that is, to those who were under the law.

When Paul was ministering to the Jews, he went along with their customs and laws just as long as nothing violated his walk in Christ. His standard was Christ, not the law. But he placed himself under the law when ministering to the Jews in order to get next to them and win their confidence and trust so he could witness to them.

2. Paul became a non-religionist to those who did not observe the law.

But note a critical fact: he does not mean he became lawless and immoral. He still obeyed the law of God; that is, he was as always under the law to Christ. He still obeyed the will of Christ, which actually includes the commandments of God and more. Paul lived as a Gentile when among them in order to get next to them and win them to Christ.

3. Paul became weak to the weak Christians.

That is, he went along with their petty rules and regulations. He refrained from doing some things that were perfectly legitimate. He conformed to their ideas and opinions just to have an open door to help them grow in Christ. He laid his personal liberty and rights aside in order to reach the new and weak Christians. He would not dare become a stumbling block to them, nor would he cause them to shut him out of their lives by offending them and thereby lose his opportunity to help them. He became as one of them in order to win them.

4. Paul clearly states his purpose for conforming to the customs and opinions of men.

Paul is declaring that he went to the extreme when necessary in order to reach people for Christ. *"I am made all things to all men, that I might by all means save some"* (v. 22). What mattered in life was not he and his rights, but the gospel. The gospel was the consuming passion of his life. Why? He wanted to do whatever he could to win people to Christ.

In 1865 an editorial in the Boston Post read, "Well-informed people know it is impossible to transmit their voices over wires, & even if it were possible, the thing would not have practical value." In 1897 Lord Kelvin said, "Radio has no future." Thomas Watson, Chairman of IBM in 1943 said, "I think there is a world market for maybe five computers." Ken Olson, President of Digital Equipment Corporation stated in 1977, "There is no reason why anyone would want a computer in their home." When the railroads were first introduced to the U.S., some folks feared that they'd be the downfall of the nation! Here's an excerpt from a letter to then President Jackson dated Jan. 31, 1829: "As you may know Mr. President, 'railroad' carriages are pulled at the enormous speed of 15 miles per hour by 'engine' which, in addition to endangering life and limb of passengers, roar and snort their way through the countryside, setting fire to crops, scaring the livestock and frightening women and children. The Almighty certainly never intended that people should travel at such breakneck speed." Grady Nut once said, "A man bought a new radio, brought it home, placed it on the refrigerator, plugged it in, turned it to WSM in Nashville TN, (home of the Grand Ole Opry), and then pulled all the knobs off. He had already tuned in all he ever wanted or expected to hear."

It is healthy for all churches, ministers and ministries to re-assess their effective relevance from time to time. In determining the direction of our relevance, I would encourage allowing the church's younger generation to weigh in heavily since they often recognize what is irrelevant in the church more than older believers do. Of course, this should be tested by the pastor and lay church leaders, but leadership will need to be flexible if we truly desire to live out Psalm 71:18 which it challenges us to "declare [God's] power to the next generation, [God's] mighty acts to all who are to come." Some churches are rutted and rather dreary because what has been will still be. While I am sure these were all fine men, they were not visionaries and they did not understand the changes that were to come to their world. As the church, let us not make the same mistake that they did. Relevance is simply discovering better ways to connect Jesus to a disconnected generation, while remaining authentic and without compromising the gospel. The book of Hebrews tells us that, *"Jesus is the same yesterday, today and forever"*. Since He personally changed my life, I know He is entirely relatable. Our job is to simply keep Him relatable throughout changing times. To do so, the church needs to pursue our mission with relevance. Our culture is radically changing before our very eyes, let us be ready for it with the Gospel of Jesus Christ. Stay open to newness. Stay open to change. Relevance does not change the message; it simply reshapes its presentation. May we never allow stylistic inflexibility to confine us and make us like the very Pharisees that were willing to crucify anyone who challenged their traditions. Let us keep our relevance if we have it and find how to become relevant once more if we have lost it!

Share It and Declare It!

Pastors if you are looking for a good deacons training piece for a few months, may I suggest you begin utilizing these chapters as tools for discussion? It has been designed for the pastor to train his church leaders in tools necessary to remain on the cutting edge as you minister to the community your serve. By taking about fifteen to twenty minutes at the beginning of every deacons or Elders meeting for such training you will help you build strong leaders within the church.

Dr. Tom Cheyney is the Founder and Directional Leader for RENOVATE National Church Revitalization Conference & Executive Director of Missions, Greater Orlando Baptist Association. Tom is a nationally recognized conference leader in church revitalization, church planting and church health. Tom has taught all over the world and is an Oxford University Distinguished Scholars Student from Midwestern Baptist Theological Seminary. Tom is the author of: *Thirty-Eight Church Revitalization Models for the Twenty First Century, Spin-Off Churches, Church Revitalizer as Change Agent, The Seven Pillars of Church Revitalization and Renewal,* and co-author of *Nuts & Bolts,* and *Preaching Towards Church Revitalization and Renewal.* Cheyney is the Executive Editor of the Church Revitalizer magazine a bi-monthly magazine which emphasizes the tools necessary to turn around one's church.

CHAPTER TWO
Lessons for the FIRST-TIME Revitalizer

By Rodney Harrison

I was recently asked, "Are Church Revitalizers born or made?" The answer was simple, since the last time I checked, 100% of us were born. Although some of our seminaries are now training individuals through specialized degree programs in revitalization, most of us are thrust into the role by circumstance rather than intent. However a person comes to the ministry of revitalization, the following lessons are designed to help and encourage you on the journey of church revitalization.

It's worse than it seems.

Accepting that the issues and challenges you face are worse then they seem might sound cynical. One needs to understand from the beginning that it took years for the church to get to this point, and the process of decline has involved many persons and a variety of circumstances. Paul helped Timothy understand this truth in 2 Timothy 3: 10-13:

> *You have followed my teaching, conduct, purpose, faith, patience, love and endurance, along with the persecutions and sufferings that came to me in Antioch, Iconium and Lystra. What persecutions I endured. Yet the Lord rescued me from them all. In fact, all those who want to live a godly life in Christ Jesus will be persecuted. Evil people and imposters will become worse, deceiving and being deceived.*

As you delve into the root causes of decline, apathy, conflict and the like, you will often find that there are "stories behind the story" that reveal additional problems. So, how should the first-time revitalizer respond to "it's worse than it seems?" By giving thanks to God for everything, even the challenges you will face. (Ephesians 5:20; Colossians 3:17; 1 Thessalonians 5:18).

Where does one start?

The temptation is to always start with outreach and evangelism. However, the correct starting place is dependent upon the health of the church. If the church is healthy, the starting place may be outreach and evangelism. Are members welcoming to newcomers and outsiders? Does the church have programs that visitors would want to experience a second time? If you were not the pastor, would this be a church you and your family would readily join? If the answers to these questions are positive, the starting point should focus on growth, outreach, evangelism and leadership development. If the answer is no, the focus should be on addressing the issues. Inviting newcomers to an unhealthy church is like inviting neighbors to dinner when you have the flu.

Does the church have spiritual or administrative issues?

It has been said never spiritualize administrative problems nor administrate spiritual problems. Most churches have issues and concerns in both areas. However, the answer for administrative problems is not always "let's pray." Administrative issues demand administrative responses, such as "let's ensure 100% of the offering is accounted for each week" or "let's identify the top three priorities for spending this month." Paul exhorted members of the church to "Pray without ceasing." This implies prayer is a natural component of all we do in ministry. However, to spiritualize administrative issues creates frustration and does not address the issue. In the same way, developing policies for spiritual issues, such as small groups that have become bee's nests for gossip is not only unwise, it will come back to sting you! Take time to identify whether problems and issues are spiritual or administrative. If the problem is long-standing, the issue may manifest itself in both, with will necessitate dealing with the spiritual and administrative aspects of the problem.

Practical Tools for Reinventing the Dying Church

Don't do it alone.

The answer to the question "how do you eat an elephant?" is often "one bite at a time." I am not an expert on elephant decomposition, but I would predict that well before one person was done with an elephant, it would no longer be eatable. The best answer is "invite the community." In the case of revitalization, that might include faithful laymen, pastors, the area director of missions or a denominational leader. Membership in a professional organization, such as the Society for Church Revitalization and Renewal, will provide a community of nurture and support. Early in the revitalization process, identify and develop a team inside and outside of the church that will support your revitalization efforts. Tom Cheyney notes that is usually takes 1000 days to turn a church around. Without a support team, most pastors will either quit, and leave the mess to someone else, or abandon the revitalization effort, joining previous leaders who gave up on God's church.

Know where you are going.

In *Pastoral Helmsmanship: A Pastor's Guide to Church Administration,* I tell the story of when a member of a growing church painted a baptismal mural with Proverbs 29:18 (Where there is no vision, the people perish—KJV). However, time and neglect caused the "W" to chip off, rending the message, "here there is no vision, the people perish." Eric Bargerhuff, in his book *The Most Misused Verses in the Bible* states, "Plain and simple, this verse is not talking about strategic planning." However, I would argue the verse does speak of having clarity of God's revelation, since knowing where you are going is vital for both the first time and seasoned revitalizer. Exploring church documents, such as the Constitution and By-Laws, both past and present, along with previous attempts to clarify vision, purpose or mission (terms I am comfortable using somewhat interchangeably) is a wise expenditure of time. Unless the church is a restart, the vision will likely be contained, even if somewhat obscure, in these documents. Vision should speak to what will be, not what is now. Being able to articulate the vision in a simple sentence conveys confidence, clarity and conviction. As you work on vision clarity, share your thoughts with your team members. As one of my mentors taught me, once you

have vision clarity, share the vision until it becomes a shared vision. Vision clarity takes time so start early, otherwise vision hijackers will seek to implant their vision in place of God's vision for His church.

Consider a covenant with God.

Given the realities of the task, consider making a commitment to the Lord to stay for three, five or seven years. One reality of ministry is that the good times are often overshadowed by the bad. Throwing in the towel is tempting when the deacons desert you, musicians are mad, group leaders are grumpy and leaders are lazy. I have found that the "greener pasture" opportunities tend to arise when things are going poorly. By making a covenant, you are saying, "Leaving prematurely is not an option. Period" Sure, the congregation may "break the covenant," but you will remain faithful on your end, even during the hard times. At the end of the journey, faithfulness to God, not earthly success should be our goal.

Dr. Rodney A. Harrison serves as Dean of Online Education and Dean of Doctoral Studies at Midwestern Baptist Theological Seminary. His ministry has focused on church revitalization and church planting. He is the author of two books on church planting and one on church administration in addition to many published articles. Harrison is an avid motorcyclist and shooting sports enthusiast. In 2011, he rode to all 50 States in 30 days using the three-minute story approach to evangelism in each state. He and his wife Julie have three grown children, Joshua, Cassandra and Gabriel.

CHAPTER THREE
Know Your Audience to Maximize Church Revitalization
By Joel R. Breidenbaugh

As I sit here writing this chapter, I am spending a few days in Sofia, Bulgaria, as my wife and I are about to take home our four-year-old adopted daughter. She knows all of a couple of English words and that is nearly the extent of our Bulgarian. While she has exhibited a fun-loving spirit through these last few days, I am sure she has been a bit frustrated at times as she tries in vain to communicate something to us.

But it didn't have to be this way. We could have been learning Bulgarian these last nine months, once we accepted her as a referral. We recently finished hosting a foreign exchange student from Ukraine, and I sat out to learn Cyrillic, the alphabet of both Ukraine and Bulgaria. I ultimately gave into my busy routine as pastor, professor and parent to keep from learning much. Oh, how I wish I would have learned more then to communicate better now!

This issue is one of the main elements of preaching—knowing your audience so you communicate more effectively. Too often I hear pastors lament how people "oooh" and "ahhh" over a guest preacher who delivers a strong message. Such a pulpit guest usually has only a few sugar sticks and he doesn't know the audience well, preaching in generalities. The local church pastor, however, has a trump card with preaching to his church—he can (get to) know his audience unlike someone filling the pulpit.

I want to share with you a few ways you can get to know your audience better so the message you preach hits a nerve with them. I do not intend to downplay the role of the Holy Spirit in applying the message, but most of us would agree He works most powerfully through the personal relationships we have cultivated.

Spend Time with Your People

One of the greatest advantages a church revitalizer has over a mega-church pastor is how much easier it is for him to get to know his audience by spending time with them. I know more than one mega-church pastor who tells other pastors not to waste time visiting with their own church people in favor of spending time finding ways to connect with the un-churched. Church revitalization and growth cannot happen without reaching out to the lost and un-churched, but a pastor, by definition, must also care for the flock the Lord has entrusted to him. So how can you spend time with your people beyond seeing them on a Sunday?

Visit Your People

As a pastor of small and medium-sized churches, I have always enjoyed visiting my church members in their homes. I learn a lot about what they value when I see their flower garden, tool shed, living room, dining room and the like. Some people place greater worth on their things than they do hosting others in their immaculate houses. Others arrange their house in such a way that the grandkids can stop by without notice and pick up right where they left off!

I often get to meet additional family members when I come into church members' homes. Such meetings allow me to connect with more people than I originally anticipated. Active church members appreciate their pastor meeting with them, and meeting their un-churched family members is a bonus for me and for them.

Stop by Their Place of Work, If Possible

Those who operate their own businesses or work for customer-relation services are almost offended if you don't stop by their workplace. Visiting their place of business gives the pastor insight into what they go through on a daily or weekly basis. It also helps you see their mission field in equipping them to reach others for Christ.

Practical Tools for Reinventing the Dying Church

Attend Their Family's Extracurricular Events

I cannot count the number of sporting events, graduations, piano recitals and comparable events I have attended over the years. I am not suggesting you spend all your time at these outings, or you will miss out on your own family. Showing up to a game and sitting with the parents and grandparents in the stands speaks volumes to others. The old adage is true: "People don't care how much you know until they know how much you care."

Have Them in Your Home

No matter how hard you try, some people will not ever invite you into their home (possibly out of fear they cannot clean it for your visit). You can, however, invite them over to your house. Though you may want to invite a couple of families over at the same time, getting to know more people, my wife and I have enjoyed hosting Sunday School classes, potluck style. After enjoying food together, I sit everyone in a large circle and have couples tell us how long they have been married and a memorable story in their lives (it is often humorous!). Everyone enjoys getting to know others better, but as their pastor, I probably get the most out of it.

Utilize Social Media to Connect with Your People

Technology provides us with many benefits unknown to previous generations. Social media sites offer elements of micro-blogging and miniature journaling. While you may not want to spend time listing many of your own life events, scrolling through what your friends and contacts have to post helps you learn what makes them tick, whether it is comments and pictures about family, vacation spots, work, favorite teams or various ideologies. Jot down occasional notes as reminders for building illustrations and application in your sermon. Although confidentiality should mark personal conversations, information on social sites is usually fair game for public use. You probably want to go the extra mile and obtain permission about sharing someone's story, especially if they are one of your church members.

In addition to scanning through other's posts, take time to "like," comment or share. People receive encouragement from others responding to their posts and pictures. It communicates your interest in their lives.

Listen, Laugh and Cry with Your People

As a pastor, you will be talking a great deal more week-in and week-out through your sermons than your members. As you spend time with others, make sure you take the lead in listening to them. If getting them to talk is difficult, use a few key questions to get them started. I like asking people how they came to know Jesus or what brought them to our church. I also inquire how couples met or find out what they do for a living. While listening to people tell their stories, you will sometimes laugh and sometimes cry, and yet always grow in your relationship with them.

Conclusion

Hopefully these suggestions will aid you in knowing your audience as you preach and shepherd. As you strengthen these relationships, you will find these people—*your people*—will grow to love you for loving them. church in need of a caring pastor.

Joel R. Breidenbaugh, Senior Pastor of First Baptist Church of Sweetwater. Prior to coming to First Baptist Sweetwater, Joel had served in the pastorate of four churches in Florida and Kentucky over 12 years. A native of Vincennes, Indiana, Joel obtained a BA in Theology from Florida Baptist Theological College, Graceville, Florida; Master of Divinity and Doctor of Philosophy (majoring in Preaching) from The Southern Baptist Theological Seminary, Louisville, Kentucky. The Lord has allowed Joel to cover different aspects of ministry, through preaching and teaching in numerous settings, including revivals, conferences, seminars, colleges and seminaries. Moreover, Joel has been privileged to share the gospel in Australia, Canada, Mexico, the Bahamas, Italy, the Vatican, Israel, Jordan, Turkey, Greece, Bulgaria and throughout much of the United States. Joel and his wife, Annthea, have five children.

CHAPTER FOUR
Regaining Relevance for Revitalization
By Mark Weible

Is your church still relevant to your city? Cities change and people change while the gospel stays the same. When your church was first started, the founding pastor and members most likely wanted the church to be relevant to the community where it was planted. They probably looked at the people with missionary vision and asked questions like, "How do we reach these people with the gospel?" Has your church's neighborhood changed so much that it is time to take a fresh look at the people you are trying to reach? Is it time to evaluate the church's relevance to the community?

"It is my judgment, therefore, that we should not make it difficult for the Gentiles who are turning to God" (Acts 15:19).

When the message of the gospel began to spread to Gentiles in the first century, church leaders realized that they were placing unnecessary religious burdens on non-Jews who were turning to Christ. To address this issue, the leaders of the early Christian Church gathered in Jerusalem to discuss whether or not to require new Gentile Christians to embrace old Jewish religious traditions. The decision was made to allow the Gentiles to worship Christ within their own cultural context. In light of the gospel of grace through faith in Christ, it would not have made sense to require the Gentiles to embrace legalistic traditions that would make it difficult for them to come to Christ. So, the church leaders removed unnecessary religious requirements and updated their practices in order to be true to the gospel while being relevant to newcomers to Christ. By considering the cultural and religious backgrounds of new people coming to Jesus, the early church was able to advance the gospel rapidly during the first century.

The Apostle Paul certainly took into account the background of his hearers whenever he shared the gospel. A classic example is when he spoke at the Aeropaus in Athens. Before speaking, Paul walked around the city and observed their objects of worship. In his message to the Athenians, Paul found

Practical Tools for Reinventing the Dying Church

common ground with his hearers by referencing the altar "to an unknown god." He used that as an opportunity to proclaim to them the one true God (Acts 17: 22-23).

In his writing to the Corinthians, Paul emphasized that he set aside his rights, privileges and preferences in order to be a more relevant preacher of the gospel:

> *"To the weak I became weak, to win the weak. I have become all things to all people so that by all possible means I might save some. I do all this for the sake of the gospel, that I may share in its blessings"* (I Corinthians 9: 22-23).

Paul made a compelling case for sharing the gospel in a culturally relevant manner. This is done, not for the sake of the hearers of the gospel, but for the sake of the gospel itself. The gospel compels us to consider the context of the hearers when sharing the good news of Christ.

Community Rediscovery

It may be necessary for your church to rediscover her community. Too often, we get too busy to take in the sights and sounds of our own neighborhoods and before long, the community changes ever so subtly that we fail to realize that the church is no longer relevant to the community. When he was in Athens, Paul walked around the city and observed the activities of the people. He saw what they were worshipping and where they lacked knowledge of the one true God. When he had the opportunity to address the people, he pointed the way to Christ.

Observation

We can be more effective at reaching our cities and neighborhoods when we take the time to get to know the area and the people all over again. My good friend, Hal Haller, loves to ride with pastors and church planters into the heart of their target communities and ask the question, "What do you see?" By asking that question, Hal is asking for an interpretation of the cultural context of the community. Many respond by saying, "I see cars, buildings, and people." Hal responds with, "What do you see?" "I see a woman with a baby stroller, a homeless man, and an elderly woman carrying a bag of groceries" the person responds. Hal asks, "What do you really see?" After further observation, one notes, "I see hurting, hopeless people living in despair and in need of the gospel of Christ." Deeper observations lead to a greater compassion for the lost and a better understanding of how to contextualize the gospel.

Demographics

In addition to subjective observation, your church may benefit from a demographic study of your community. You may be able to request this from your denominational office or you can purchase a demographic survey directly from a vendor such as The Percept Group (perceptgroup.com). A good demographic study will combine census data with psychographic profiles of population segments within your defined study area. This information, combined with your own observations can help you to gain a greater understanding of the people that you are trying to reach.

Assessment

A Community Needs Assessment could be helpful for discovering ways that your church can help meet the needs of people and community service agencies serving your city. A CNA involves church members interviewing officials with local government and community service agencies. Participants ask these community leaders about the purpose of the organizations that they lead, how they serve the community and how the church can help. This process can not only help the church better understand the needs of the community, but also serve to create connections of opportunity for service.

Survey

Another tool for community rediscovery is the community survey. This can be done online or through **direct mail,** however community surveys are most effective when they are done face to face. Depending on the area, these surveys can be

Practical Tools for Reinventing the Dying Church

conducted in businesses, residential areas or both. The idea is to make direct contact with people and ask them about what is important to them, their impressions of the neighborhood and what they would like to see changed. Bob Logan, author of the Church Planter's Toolkit, suggests asking what radio station they listen to. This will give some insight into the music preferences of the people living in the area. When conducting a community survey, bear in mind that the interaction is more important than the information. Interviewers don't want to be in a rush to gather information and move on the next person. The person conducting the interview may very well be the only person that a community member has met from the local church and this time can also be used for relationship building.

Designing Ministry

After observations, interviews and data gathering the information needs to be compiled into a presentable format for discussion. The data should be shared with a planning team and, eventually, the church body. With a better view of the community, you can start with a blank slate. unproductive or ineffective programs and adding new ministries.

Mark Weible is the Strategic Director of the Renovate National Church Revitalization Conference and the Church Planting Director for the Greater Orlando Baptist Association. He joined the team in 2002. Previously he served as an associate director of missions, pastor, radio station operations manager, youth pastor, and children's home house parent, all in Texas. Mark's certifications include: Executive Coach, Church Planter Assessor, Natural Church Development Coach, DISC Coach, Search Engine Optimizer Google Advertising Specialist, and Lead Like Jesus Leadership Development Facilitator. Mark is married to Tammy and they have four children; three boys and one girl.

CHAPTER FIVE
Where Does Church Revitalization Begin?
By Jim Grant

The topic of Church Revitalization has been a subject of interest for several years now. Most people are familiar with Olsen's *American Church in Crisis* and an often-quoted statistic about plateaued, dying and dead churches. While the information from Olsen may be a little outdated, the question of what to do about the epidemic is still relevant for anyone in such a ministry position.

I have done enough research on the topic to realize that every denomination is struggling with how to stop its churches from closing their doors. I discovered that there are multiple reasons why a church will die; to include the location, past church history and leadership issues. As a result of the emphasis given to the number of churches closing, various philosophies, approaches and tools have been developed in hopes of finding the root cause of the epidemic.

I appreciate the high level of interest and energy given by so many including my own denomination to find a solution. Church Revitalization does not have an easy solution. There are too many variables to investigate and filter through to determine a "common cause" among the churches. While there are no quick fixes or answers, when a church does find new life again the results are remarkable.

Some of the variables that must be taken into account before starting any church revitalization project include the age of the church, the age of the congregation, past church history (successes and failures), community demographics (growing or declining in population), and whether or not current leadership is capable of leading the process.

Often Church Revitalization enthusiasts are eager to do the research, conduct community and church surveys and crunch the data in hopes of uncovering the hidden secret to turning around a failing church. In our current technological age a researcher can find just about any information to diagnose a perceived condition within a church. The conclusion may point to a problem that is geographical as well as spiritual. Do not misunderstand me, there must be sufficient homework accomplished before settling on a course of action. Life has taught me that one must be careful with statistical information alone. Church revitalization is not a one-dimensional issue.

If a church is to begin a revitalization process, it is absolutely essential to know where to start but even more important to know where the Church is headed. Church revitalization inherently carries with it the idea that at some point the church that is now languishing was at another point successful and alive. Having said that, the question comes to mind – What does it mean to have a successful past? If a church cannot identify a time when it was healthy and accomplishing Kingdom work, then it may need to start with a Strategic Planning Team to develop for the very first time a clear vision or concept of what it means to be a New Testament church.

Church revitalization is about causing renewal within the life of redeemed people and within the church's current dilemma. Revitalization is not revival; it is more than revival. I have pastored four churches. I may not be an expert, but I have found some steps that will help determine a successful church transformation.

First, *every church is different:* its context, its people and its particular ministry for the Kingdom of God. There have been enough attempts at reviving dying churches to provide a plethora of books documenting the success story.

Secondly, *revitalization is absolutely difficult work.* While reading these stories, one quickly learns that it is a difficult process. As with any work within the church, one can expect opposition and discouragement along the way. Church revitalization requires diplomacy and perseverance.

Thirdly, *revitalization requires the right leader.* Even though so many churches are experiencing warning signs of decline and death, not every pastor is a revitalizer.

Revitalization is as much about the pastor/leadership as it is about the overall church. There are churches that would rather die than change; there are also pastors that would rather change pastorates than embark on the struggles of changing a church. Scripture is filled with examples of resistance to God's will, in particular the nation of Israel. Often a position of comfort is sought. This should not sound so strange; individuals and church naturally acquiesce to a point of their comfort.

In a church situation where revitalization is being considered, before all the research and studies are done, leadership must answer one question: Are they the ones to attempt this revitalization? This may sound like a dumb question, but in reality, this must be the first investigative point. Long before thoughts of studies and demographic analysis is attempted, there has to be clear direction from the Lord Jesus that the leadership is called to the work of revitalization. Specifically, is the pastor the right person? This question cannot be easily answered. According to Luke 14:28, before attempting a work you must consider the cost beforehand. If the pastor/leadership is not willing to invest at least five to seven years towards the work, do not start. The work will go unfinished and the people will become further discouraged, hindering any future work. Many reading this article now are trying to determine if they are called to revitalization. This is a pertinent question that must be asked with a peace and clear understanding from God. Word of caution: revitalization will not be like anything you have done before!

The bible character of Joshua is an example to many potential revitalizers. There was much that Joshua had to consider about his new position as leader of Israel. As ministers of the Gospel, we are under obligation to the One who called us. Right now, many pastors find themselves in less than the best of church health situations. Our faithfulness in the difficult times will be a reflection of God's preparation of us for the task. Pastors, we are in difficult times. It is our watch and we must be found faithful.

Joshua had to reflect on what God had been doing in his life. Joshua was a valiant warrior. He had experienced great victories and witnessed the powerful presence of God. While he was part of the disappointing "committee' that chose not to enter the Promised Land, he didn't quit or give up. He stayed faithful for forty years in the position of Captain of the Israeli army. Before Moses dies, he is anointed as heir apparent to lead Israel to the Promise Land. This is quite a change of positions, no longer is he the executor of the plan, he is the Vision Caster. Wonderful words of encouragement and challenge come from God to Joshua. (Joshua 1:1-9)

The leadership changed but the goal remained the same. Forty years in the Wilderness did not alter God's goal. Israel was always supposed to inhabit the Promise Land. God still commands churches to fulfill the Great Commission. Pastors and leadership will change, but God always remains the same. Those encouraging words from God "As I was with Moses, so I will be with You (Josh 1:5) are for us.

Joshua was given a task to do that had the outcome already determined. The LORD said "I am giving this land to them." (Josh 1:2) There would be fighting, but Joshua was told that no man would be able to stand against what God was doing.

Joshua did not let the circumstances and past dictate the future obedience and work of the Lord. We may all find ourselves from time to time in situations that seem impossible – but do not fret; God is still on His throne and we have been called to shepherd His Church. Three times in Joshua 1, Joshua is told "Be strong and courageous." While it is imperative that churches and pastors remember what happened in the past, they cannot let it paralyze them. Now Joshua could have struggled in the shadows of Moses or he could accept the new role as "Valiant Leader." Additionally, Joshua had fought many battles in the typical manner of warfare. Right from the beginning, Joshua and the people had to trust in un-orthodox ways – God's ways.

So where does Church revitalization begin? It begins with pastors. Before a pastor embarks on revitalization, he must look at himself. Leadership must switch from being caretakers to risk takers. There are many qualities that have been used to help identify if someone is a church revitalizer. God looks for only one – being a man after God's own heart. God will build His church. If God has called you to revitalization, do not look for another church. Church revitalization is difficult, but when God is in the church, the church has a future. There are no easy answers and no quick fixes. God called us to shepherd His church, so let's model our own Good Shepherd and be willing to lay down our life for the sheep.

Jim Grant Serves as the Lead Pastor of Heartland Baptist Church in Alton, Illinois. He is a veteran with 25 years of service in the Air Force. His extensive travels, while in the military, allowed him the unique ability to have served in the full spectrum of churches, styles, and health. He has a M.Div. with Biblical Languages from Southwestern Baptist Theological Seminary, and a D.Min. from Midwestern Baptist Theological Seminary with a concentration on Church Revitalization. Jim is a frequent contributor to the Church Revitalizer Magazine and a regular presenter at the Renovate National Church Revitalization Conference. He has been married to his wife for 39 years and they have two daughters and four grandchildren.

CHAPTER SIX
Survival Tips for a Young Pastor
By Rob Arnold

At a recent denominational meeting, I was told that a church in our community terminated a young pastor after only six months. News of this kind always brings a twinge of sorrow to my heart, especially when it involves a young minister. Inevitably, more experienced pastors will comment that if the young pastor had simply heeded some friendly advice or recognized the warning signs he could have avoided his loss.

The probability that a young pastor will lose his job is unusually high. According to Thom Rainer, about 1.5 percent of pastors have lost their jobs each year due to forced terminations,2 which is not terribly high. If, however, 75 to 89 percent of your church is over 60, you are three times more likely to fire the pastor, and if you have virtually no adults under 35, the church is even more likely to force terminate the pastor. Additionally, Rainer warns that if the pastor is under 30 years old, the church is three and half times more likely to let the pastor go, and 'three and half times' is a huge statistical variance.3 Rainer's statistics serve as a warning to young pastors and prompts the question, "What can a young pastor do to improve his odds?" I have been in the ministry for 31 years and had some narrow escapes of my own, so I have five tips or suggestions for you to consider for improving your odds at surviving and thriving in your first years as a pastor.

Do your homework.

An ounce of prevention is worth a pound of cure. Knowing a church's history before you arrive can spare you a pound of heartache. Their track record serves as an excellent indicator on how a church will treat you. Do not fall into the trap of being so

---

2 Rainer, Thom, *Church Staff: Some Observations,* ThomRainer.com, Sept. 07, 2011.

3 Rainer, Thom, *Eight Warning Signs for Forced Terminations of Pastors,* ThomRainer.com, May 12, 2012.

eager that you fail to discriminate between churches that respect their pastors and the churches with histories of serial pastor abuse. Contact the associational director. Talk to pastors in the community, and if possible, talk to one or two of the previous pastors. Keep in mind, though, that there are two sides to every story. The previous pastors' mistakes may have laid landmines that will derail the effectiveness of the next pastor. A search committee will neglect to share the history that subtly affects every area of church life, so unearthing that history may be the difference between your failure and success.

Make a long-term commitment.

Successful church renovators avoid the "quick fix" and make long-term commitments. Know the church's strengths and weaknesses and count the cost. Remember that any great work will require a substantial investment of time and energy, because nothing of eternal value happens in the Kingdom of God without blood, sweat, and tears. Are you going to be a hireling who runs from problems, or the shepherd who loves and feeds God's sheep? As you go into a new church, do not make the stipulation that significant change must happen immediately. Change takes time, and older churches are weary of young pastors with unrealistic expectations who use their church as a steppingstone to "better" churches with more people and larger salaries.

Earn the trust of the church members.

Being the pastor of the church does not automatically imbue you with their trust or authority. If you assume that your authority is automatic with your position, you will discover you are sadly mistaken. Trust in a church must be earned. Furthermore, if the church has suffered through a string of ineffectual pastors, it will be more difficult for them to trust you. To complicate the situation, usually there are lay leaders who have stuck with the church through the hard times, and they may possess de facto pastoral authority. If they are reluctant to yield that authority to you, you will have your work cut out for you. You must be willing, therefore, to communicate in word and

Practical Tools for Reinventing the Dying Church

deed a sincere love for the church, a competence in church polity, and a desire to maintain Christian unity. If you do so over time, you will slowly earn their trust and assume the mantle of authority.

Move slowly when presenting new ideas.

When you attempt to lead an old, established church through change and revitalization, timing and your packaging are critical. An idea, no matter how great, is doomed to fail if packaged and presented poorly. The most common mistake you can make is to move too fast. Remember, a member may think about church once a week, while you think about church every day. Since this is true, a rule of thumb is that for every day you spend ruminating on a new idea, give the congregation one additional week to mull it over. Consequently, if you spend one week pounding out a new idea, allow seven to eight weeks for the congregation to assimilate the same idea. This involves an open-door policy of allowing them to talk to you in private and ask questions. You may think this is excessive, but church members need more time to digest new ideas.

Additionally, present your ideas one at a time. If you overwhelm a congregation with new ideas and they will reject them all. Be assured, you must become an expert in timing and packaging. Your ideas may be flawless, but package them poorly and present too quickly and you will experience heartache and failure.

Recognize the warning signs.

Churches do not intentionally set out to fire young pastors, but problems naturally arise, and if the young pastor and leaders cannot resolve conflict constructively, a forced termination looms on the horizon. A floundering ship will send up flares, and a church in troubled waters will give off warning signs. Learn to recognize, therefore, those warning signs and be proactive. Decisive measures can calm fears and keep conflict from escalating. Successful pastors and church revitalizers realize that churches are full of imperfect people with personal agendas. There are power brokers, sacred cows, and the dysfunctional baggage from previous pastorates in every church. Every congregation, no matter how godly, has potential minefields that the new pastor must learn to navigate if he is to survive and prosper. Godly pastors will seek the help and guidance of more experienced pastors or denominational leaders. In contrast, however, if you refuse to seek advice and you ignore the warning signs, you will exhaust the patience and good will of the godliest church. Your ability to adapt, seek help, and respond constructively to the warning signs will determine your level of effective leadership.

You can add to this list, I am sure, and obviously, these suggestions are contingent on your prayer life, your level of personal integrity, and your time in God's Word; but these five suggestions can help you thrive and flourish in an aging church that is in desperate need of strong pastoral leadership, change, and revitalization.

Rob Arnold is the pastor of Lockhart Church in Orlando and an occasional contributor to the Church Revitalizer Magazine. Rob has spoken at the Renovate National Church Revitalization Conference many times and is a strong leader of a church experiencing revitalization and renewal.

CHAPTER SEVEN
Relevant Preaching and the Revitalization of the Church
By Paul E. Smith

Some years past I was leading a conference with Aubrey Malphurs on Church Planting. He spent two days talking to everyone about their structure, style, systems, statements, strategies, and staff of a church planting. The last day, I was to address preaching. Make no mistake about this, "THEY CAME TO HEAR AUBREY". Yet, as I stood on that day to begin I said something like this, "If your structure, style, systems, statements, strategies, and staff are in place, perfect and pleasing, yet you have NOTHING TO SAY, how long will they stay"? At least for the moment I had their attention. Perhaps as I have yours now. As we try to revitalize the Church, I want to address some of the things about preaching in this day that may be a bit controversial, and anti-cultural, but extremely necessary as you fight the good fight of faith in leading your church to be what God intends for her to be, the Bride.

I want to address some of the relevant issues in preaching as well the relevancy of preaching in our efforts to revitalize the church. The question I want to begin with is this one, "Can preaching be a defining moment in the lives of people today"? We know from a historical perspective that preaching can be a defining moment. From the prophets of the Old Testament giving a "thus says the Lord" word to the evangelist and pastors of the New Testament providing a current event "thus says the Lord" word, preaching has provided many defining moments for individuals, communities, cultures, and countries (those no longer in existence as well as those still in existence today). I know you believe preaching to be a defining Moment. I know you pray, plan, practice and prepare to be used by God in your preaching so that it will be a defining moment. So, let's delve into this deeper. Is preaching an event or is it an experience for you and your people? I'm not trying to provide semantics, but instead trying to get us to think through the potential difference. I have been to events and I have experienced events. I have been to numerous graduation ceremonies in my tenure as a pastor. I have preached them, hosted them, sat through them, endured them, and even enjoyed some. Yet this past May, I sat in a graduation ceremony in Iowa that brought me to tears as I watched the processional, presentations of degrees, and even the speakers address. Lara and I watched our 23-year-old, NCAA Wrestling Athlete, walk across the stage to receive the business degree he earned in FOUR YEARS. Still not sure if I was crying because of his accomplishment or the cost. But, I was sure crying! What made this event different from others that caused it to be such an emotional experience that I cried? Simply put, IT WAS PERSONAL!

I am concerned today that preaching has become less personal. In revitalizing a church there are numerous issues that "the people" have with the change that is occurring in "THEIR" Church. Preaching is one of the best and most effective ways to ease those changes in the church when preaching is personal. I, of course, am in no way speaking about attacking personal issues in the church. I call that "pot shot" preaching. A person stands behind the anointed shining silver lectern these days, rather than the Holy Wood of the olden days, and feels completely comfortable taking "pot shots" at local politics, people's habits, or even problems the pastor may have with certain people. Making preaching personal is letting the Bible address the issues, events, changes needed, relationship issues, and even structural issues with BIBLICAL RELEVANCY. The pathos and ethos of the early presenters of the Scriptures was evident because of the way they received it and were required to live it. I suggest that we need to find a way to receive the word with freshness today, not as if it was "old news", but as "GOOD NEWS". A quick look back into the scriptures as well as history indicates that those who preached the word did so with liveliness, emotion, personality, authority, freedom, sensitivity, seriousness, zeal, warmth, urgency, persuasion, and power. The business model presented to a different generation informs us and instructs us as to "what people will listen to and what they won't listen to", and many today are preaching designer sermons based on their audience rather than dynamic sermons based on the audible hearing of God (yes, it should be so loud you can't miss it) as to what they should say. For preaching today to be relevant it must be personal.

Practical Tools for Reinventing the Dying Church

Relevant preaching today must not only be personal, IT MUST BE PRACTICAL. An irrelevant word is a waste of everyone's time. I have told my people numerous times if they ever want to drive me to my prayer room and fasting, as they have to do is say, "Pastor, that word wasn't very relevant (practical) today. Making your messages practical is not putting them in the form of "How to" or "What for". To revitalize the Church, we have to revitalize our preaching to make it practical. I know many will argue that the Bible is irrelevant for today. I think those who make such an argument are being irreverent to their calling and commission. I could spend time, although 1200 words won't allow me, giving you scripture references where the Bible in its own time period was culturally, politically, socially, emotionally, and financially perceived to be irrelevant. But remember, it establishes, promotes, and teaches about how to live LIFE in a NEW KINGDOM... God's Kingdom. And its practical, relevant, ways are only such in God's kingdom. Our task, calling and commitment in revitalization is to preach and passionately believe that living according to God's kingdom principles will result in kingdom come reality. Aren't you amazed at how many people believe reality TV over the kingdom reality of the Scriptures? I even see and hear more sermon titles from reality TV. Imagine, preaching a reality sermon on John the Baptist. The eating of wild locust, honey, and the dressing in camel hair could make even an episode of Survivor look lame. Pray, fast, and meditate to make your preaching practical to the people from a Kingdom's perspective not a cultural one.

The last issue I have space to address in this article is this: relevant preaching today must not only be personal and practical, IT MUST BE POWERFUL. Powerful preaching is not determined by emotions, tenor, and volume. Yes, those do play a role at times. Powerful preaching is taking the Word of God and presenting it to the people so they can personally encounter and experience God. We have judged far too long the effectiveness of our preaching by those who "accept" God's word. I encourage you to look at the times the Bible mentions about those who "didn't accept" the word and the consequences that ensue.

It seems THE CHURCH is always trying to hone, re-create, change, struggle, and adapt with the demands placed upon her by society and culture. Through the years many changes have occurred from times of services, length of service, days of the week, places where the church meets, songs (remember the worship wars), decor, stain-glass vs no glass, Starbucks vs Folgers (read the book), and many more. I remember a reference in a movie years ago that made a powerful point as to the media's involvement in our country and simply said of Ronald Reagan, "No wonder they elected an actor as the President". If we are not careful, perhaps the same could, should, and will be said about the pulpits of our churches. Such a charge from the world may not be avoided. However, for us to avoid such a charge from God, we must, as his original presenters of the Word did, make the scriptures relevant so we can revitalize HIS church.

Paul Smith is the Lead Pastor of Life Church, in Mandeville, LA. He is a leader, visionary, and teacher. He is a widely sought after conference speaker, Bible Teacher, and motivational presenter. He has traveled all over the Americas, North, South, and Central, teaching, preaching, and strategizing with church revitalizers, church planters, ministers, and leaders of denominations.

CHAPTER Eight
"Danger, Will Robinson!": Dangerous Threats to the Church Revitalization Movement
By Terry Rials

One could hardly deny that there is a grand new movement in the American church, which crosses geographical, socio-economic, and even denominational boundaries. Interest in the Church Revitalization Movement can be found predominantly among the smallest churches, which are struggling to survive; but there is growing interest in the movement with the leaders of the largest churches, as these leaders have noticed a halt in their church's growth. In short, the smaller the church, the more interest exists in revitalization with laypeople; conversely, the larger the church, the more the interest is found with the church's leadership.

Perhaps not since the beginnings of the Church growth movement has there been such an excitement among church leaders about the prospects for the church. Admittedly, not every church leader has embraced this new movement, but a substantial percentage see the importance of addressing the decline of the existing church.

It is important to keep the Church Revitalization Movement going and not allow this work to fall prey to the errors that will kill it. If we are wise, we will look to the mistakes of past movements and put safeguards in place now to prevent the premature death of the Church Revitalization movement. I would like to enumerate six specific dangers to the movement.

The first danger, as we learned from the Missional Church Movement, is that any true movement in His church must be founded upon a correct Christology. If we get our theology wrong, our ecclesiology will be wrong. Alan Hirsch and Michael Frost say this well in *The Shape of Things to Come*. They argue that our Christology informs our missiology, which in turn determines our ecclesiology. If we allow our notions of what the church should be to taint our understanding of what the church should do, we are not authentic disciples of Christ. In essence, if the church's concentration is on its forms, leadership style, governance, furniture, worship style, Bible translation, timing of its services, etc., it is not concentrating on the headship of Christ and His mission for the church. Put simply, how can the church be the church if a church does not do what the church does? What we do and what the church looks like must be based upon our theological beliefs.

A plethora (and I use that word intentionally) of mistakes were made in the Church Growth Movement, and yet it is still with us. One of these mistakes is the second danger – an unhealthy concentration on numbers for numbers' sake. Wide is not deep. Bill Hybels confessed that while his church became broad in numbers, it was not composed of vast numbers of healthy disciples. As an alternative, we should concentrate on developing discipleship in the church. Wouldn't we as church leaders prefer to have a smaller group of dedicated disciples than a larger group of shallow attendees? Church leaders always desire more, that is a natural desire, but how we get more is also a critical concern. In the case of the church, the ends do not justify the means. *How* we get there is just as important as *getting* there.

The third danger affronting the Church Revitalization Movement is one that plagued other movements – the rampant development of the personal interests of those who led it. In the past, key leaders in thriving churches received an inordinate amount of praise and recognition. They were invited to write books, speak at conferences, and teach in academia. Many of these leaders prospered professionally and financially from their success. This is what Thomas O'Dea called the "dilemma of mixed motivation."[4] Not that any of those things is wrong or improper in itself, however they can be improper motivation, and they often lead to squabbling among leaders about the meaning of words (e.g. *revitalization, renewal, refreshing*) and the future course of the movement. The surprising thing that I have discovered while working in the field of church revitalization is

---

4 Thomas F. O'Dea, "Five Dilemmas in the Institutionalization of Religion" in *Sociology and the Study of Religion* (New York: Basic Books, Inc., 1970), 244.

that no one person has all the answers. Like a jigsaw puzzle, there are a thousand pieces to the complete picture and no one has all the pieces. I genuinely like the personalities who are leading the Church Revitalization Movement, but I intend to help keep all of them firmly grounded in humility, so that the only entity that prospers is the church, and the only one glorified is the Lord Jesus Christ.

The fourth danger I mentioned briefly before. One way that a movement begins to wane is when it is moved into the academy. Church Revitalization is a ministerial practice that involves copious amounts of prayer, personal sacrifice, and personal leadership development. I confess that I went to the seminary to understand church revitalization, earning my doctorate in that concentration. However, I can assure you that academia is not a cure for pastoral frustration; the demands of academic pursuits may take a serious toll on your ministry; it did in my setting. Allow me to say it this way – church revitalization cannot be *just* an academic pursuit. Instead, it is an applied ministry pursuit, requiring the heart of a pastor and countless hours of hard work on the church field, not just in the church office.

The fifth danger occurs when methodology and pragmatism, rather than the dictates of scripture, determine the movement's course. Concentrating on the process of revitalization can even lead to *sequentialism*, the belief that if one follows linear, step-by-step processes, then revitalization will occur in the church. It is common for church leaders, many of whom are excellent strategic planners, to think, plan, and act in sequential steps. This kind of thinking will be deadly to the Church Revitalization Movement. Our job as church leaders is not to *grease the machinery* in order to keep the organization going and growing; instead, our job is to seek first the kingdom of God and His righteousness. Our job as leaders is not to lay out step-by-step directions for other to follow. Our job is to lead others back to the heart of God and trust His leadership in their lives. If the church comes back to life and vitality, it will be a spiritual process, and not a mechanical one.

The sixth and final danger is obvious to me. If the Church Revitalization Movement is to survive and thrive, we cannot ignore the work of God in the process. Let me emphasize, there is a work that we do (revitalization) and a work that only God can do (revival). I define *revitalization* as the work we do to ensure the conditions of God are met for revival, so that the people of God are prepared when He begins to move. We need a genuine, Spirit-led revival in the church – we need God to do what only God can do, revive the church! I believe in the importance and need for both revitalization and revival in the Lord's church today. Revitalization is preparatory to revival and subsequent to it. Borrowing from G. Campbell Morgan, we must put up our sail and wait for the wind to blow. When the wind begins to blow, we make use of the wind and allow it to drive us.

I am not a prophet, nor a son of a prophet, but I predict that there will be difficult days ahead for the Church Revitalization Movement, primarily because the enemy will be actively attacking those associated with it. This should not dissuade us from the work at hand, if anything it should compel us to press on with an even greater fervor. we should take our enemy's opposition as proof that we are on the right track. If we are wise, we will recognize the dangers that lay ahead. Those who stand in the pulpit should know this intuitively, but if not, let me remind you again. Sailors who stand out on the pulpit of the ship were placed there to recognize the dangers under the surface of the water as the ship comes into the harbor, and to warn
others about that danger. May we as church leaders watch vigilantly for these dangers and stand ready to ring the bell.

Dr. Terry Rials serves as the Senior Pastor of the Crestview Baptist Church of Oklahoma City, and he serves as the Church Revitalization Team Leader for Capital Baptist Association in Oklahoma. He is a frequent conference speaker and teacher, leading church revitalization efforts in his state and nationally. Terry is the co-author of *The Nuts and Bolts of Church Revitalization* and a regular speaker at the Renovate.

CHAPTER NINE
Successful Student Pastors Have Well Defined Expectations
By Drew Cheyney

Whether you are aware of it or not, we all have expectations placed upon us. When you are born, it is expected that you will one day grow up. When you are married, it is expected of you to be the best husband or wife you can be. As you grow older, it is expected that one day you will pass "six feet under." In fact, pastoring people comes with its expectations too! For example, have you ever taken a job where you were sold the moon and recognized when you got into the thick of the mess because there was more expected of you than you realized? Subsequently, this may come from wisdom, or it may come from being blindsided before myself, but have you ever asked this question from your leadership & church: *What is Expected of Me?* Such a random thing to ask because we all have job expectations, right? For instance, you are probably expected to grow your ministry, see students accept Jesus into their lives, impact your community, and hang out with students and leaders. But exactly how big does someone think your ministry needs to be? How many lives need to be changed for your leadership style to be seen as impactful? What does community impact mean specifically? And the biggest one, how many students and leaders is seen as *enough* for you to meet the expectation? Seem a little over detailed? Well if you have ever been in a leadership position where not knowing these measures has burned you in the past, then those details may just save you some sanity and certain stress.

Currently, I am in my seventh year of pastoring students, and if I would have had the wisdom to ask clearly what was expected of me in every place I have led, I would have stayed a whole lot saner in ministry. Instead I did what the majority of student pastors do, I let surface answers and lack of specifics fly because when it comes to student ministry, what else matters but impacting students? Well, the answer is actually A LOT! Marc Devries, Pastor and Author, says this about expectations, "If you want your youth worker to succeed, define what "success" will look like. Most youth workers think they've been hired to build relationships with students and develop creative programs. Few realized they've been hired to run complex organizations."[5]

Consequently, the problem in some of our situations is that few of us are *clearly* ever told what matters most to the ministries we are leading. So when we step into situations where we have to be master marketers, befriend certain "E.G.R." elders, or meet numerical numbers we are unaware of, we become overwhelmed by what we wish we had known sooner. Devries continues in his book by saying, "seldom do expectations rear their heads in the context of a calm, clarifying discussion. Most often they come in the form of multiplying complaints that they leave the youth worker feeling as if he or she was lied to somewhere in the interview process."[6] So again, here is the question that matters most in whatever year, position, or church you are in: *What is Expected of Me… Really?*

Right now I am leading at a church in California who was very upfront with me about what they expected: I was brought in to increase attendance, implement our church's vision, develop a strong and deep leadership infrastructure, figure out any and all systematic or structural barriers which are inhibiting our student ministry overall, and develop an Associate Pastor who has the potential to one day take my job when God decides my time in student ministry is over. Sound pretty specific? Here was the best part of the agreement, I was told from the very beginning that our numbers were to reflect 10% of what our adult attendance averages weekly. I was told not to change anything or make drastic moves within the first 6 months so I could get to know our culture, team, and people better before doing so. And best of all, I was given a time frame for those expectations too! Do you know what that has done for me? It has given me a clear picture of what is exactly expected of my leadership role. Is it perfect? NO! But what it is, is a clear goal, path, vision, and expectation that I can completely get behind because I legitimately know what I agreed to walk into.

---

5 Devries, Mark. *Sustainable Youth Ministry*. Downers Grove: InterVarsity Press, 2008. Print.

6 Ibid, 105.

Practical Tools for Reinventing the Dying Church

So here is the hard part, do you know what is expected of you? Have you had conversations that lead to you getting exact answers? Whether you have done it right in the past or not, the important thing is that you have those answers at your disposal now! Why? Because knowing what is expected of you allows you to walk comfortably in your own skin, which also lets you problem solve, create, plan, and lead your ministries more effectively.

A former lead pastor of mine wrote a book a couple years ago designed as an impassioned plea to fellow pastors to "check themselves at the front door" when it came to leading and pastoring people; and in this book he wrote this: "an amazing sense of freedom comes with becoming secure in our own skin, secure in who we are, and secure in what God has called us to be and do."[7] I do not know about you, but there is nothing I want more in my calling then to be able to be the husband, leader, & man God designed me to be, and knowing what is expected of my leadership position helps me be those things. So ask yourself again: *What is Expected of Me?*

Knowing When to Pull the Trigger for Church Revitalization in Student Ministry

Revitalization is a scary word for a lot of Student Ministries because it means something that no leader likes to admit or, for that matter, truthfully wants to hear. It means that something used to work in the past and for whatever reason(s) *"it"* no longer makes the kind of impact "it" once did. So words like decline, patterns, and dying are by no means any leader's favorite descriptions to use when talking about the ministries we lead. Nevertheless, there are churches that some of us led, or are currently leading that are avoiding this very topic. Knowing when to pull the trigger on revitalization is a big deal not only for student ministries that are currently dying off, but also for the Student Ministries that are right on the cusp of potentially tilting either way. Now I am not a huge list maker, but if you

---

[7] Lovejoy, Shawn. *The Measure of Our Success: An Impassioned Plea to Pastors.* Grand Rapids: Baker Books, 2012.

find yourself hearing the following statements frequently, you may want to start having some very honest conversations about revitalizing your student ministry.

1. "Almost no one comes to our Student Ministry anymore."

If you have led anywhere on a church staff, you have heard the saying "we count people because people count." As a staff member, attendance is something we celebrate, count, and measure every week. And while numbers fluctuate throughout the course of a year, consistent patterns of decline in the areas of reaching students should be a huge concern. You can make groups seem bigger by changing environments, you can have your huge event that brings in your biggest number of the year, but when each week your leaders, students, and even you start to hear this statement, it is time to ask the question- WHY?

You and I may come to the conclusion that it is environments, or programming, maybe even it's our group structures or leadership that is the reason people are not coming, but there are typically one fundamental reason students stop caring about your student ministry: *lack of authentic community*. Students attend things they find value in, and for the majority of students, any place that makes them feel like their noticed, valued, and matter will always hold a spot in their heart and therefore their weekly schedule. So, is the reason "almost no one comes to our student ministry anymore" really more about the lack of programming, environments, or whatever else, or is it more simple than that? Carey Nieuwhof, author and lead pastor of Connexus Church, says this: "Nobody should be able to out-community the local church. You can make a legitimate argument that one of the reasons behind the explosive growth of the first-century church was because of the way they loved each other and the world. Love should be a defining characteristic of the local church. If we loved the way Jesus loved, people would **line up out the door**."[8] Maybe part of the reason our ministries will one day be in decline if we are not careful, is because the

---

8 Nieuwhof, Carey. *Lasting Impact*. Cumming: The rethink Group, Inc. 2015. Print.

DNA of our ministries is not a great representation of the way Jesus had community with people.

2. "But _____ is what we have always done."

Ever heard this one before? You snicker because all pastors have heard this one at some point or another. In fact, it is a very common theme for those of us who have taken over any areas of ministry at any point or time. We all know getting people to buy into change is hard, but it is those of us who master getting people to care about healthy change that may never have to pull the trigger on revitalization from the ground up. In his book *Lasting Impact*, Carey Nieuwhof says this, "The honest truth is, most churches, people, and organizations struggle with change. Change is hard because by default, we cling to the status quo. Typically, people change when the pain associated with the status quo becomes greater than the pain associated with change."[9] Churches that choose to keep doing what they have always done are essentially deciding to live with the consequences of stagnation, decline, and decay.[10]

3. "It's not as fun as it used to be"

This is a no brainer for most of us, but while Jesus is 100% the reason for what we do in the local church, your church cannot just sing songs, teach a message, and think that will be the kind of student ministry that moves teenagers towards Jesus. Student ministries that stand the test of times do so because their idea of "fun" is consistently evolving. Events, small groups, summer camps, and weekly engagement are the places students start to lower their walls and enjoy the company around them. Student ministries that do not take the time to have legitimate fun each week with their students will eventually become non-existent. Students will always stay for something that engages them, but if we continue to rob them of fun memories and moments they had while in our ministries then we may need to

---

9 Nieuwhof, Carey. *Lasting Impact: 7 Powerful Conversations That Will Help Your Church Grow*. Cumming: The rethink Group, Inc. 2015. Print.
10 Ibid, 146.

consider if our approach to inspiring students to live more like Jesus is actually working [F.Y.I.: Jesus had fun too].

4. "I never really found out what my NEXT STEP was."

Reaching our students is a huge part of getting them into the doors of our ministries, but what keeps them connected is the way we help them navigate through their spiritual journey. The best way to do so is by helping your students get connected in areas they are passionate about serving in, encouraging them to attend mission trips, challenging them to have a personal relationship with God, AND SO MUCH MORE! However, none of this is possible if you and I do not care about executing our follow-up strategy really well. Reaching people is so important, but consistent follow-up with our students will not only help them excel, but it will also help them not lose their faith by the time they leave for College as well.

5. "At least those who remained are "high quality" people."

Lee Kricher, Pastor of Amplify Church and Author of *For A New Generation* writes this in his new book: "Our church had accepted as truth a statement that is popular with declining churches: "God is more concerned with quality than quantity."[11] Just like Lee realized, when your church begins to care less that lost people are not attending and starts to care more that at least the people who are coming are "high quality" then you need to come to the realization that what Jesus has called us to do is not being accomplished. Depth and personal growth are great things to strive for, but we are supposed to be reaching lost people in our calling, not just reaching Christians.

We all have our "things" when it comes to the ministries we lead, but at some point each and every leader has to be making the kind of decisions that allow for people's hearts to be impacted. I know that the world we live in is not the "church world" of old where people felt guilty if they did not attend, where families made church part of their weekly schedule instead

---

11 Kricher, Lee. *For A New Generation: A Practical Guide For Revitalizing Your Church*. Grand Rapids: Zondervan. 2016. Print.

Practical Tools for Reinventing the Dying Church

of a thing they do if they have time, but that is why this conversation matters. It is the churches and student ministries that are not afraid to have this conversation that last through the changes in times and generations. Student pastors maybe for you, it's time to have a conversation about changing the way we do church and figuring out new ways to breathe life, energy, and excitement into the student ministries where we serve.

Drew Cheyney is student pastor at Neighborhood Church, CA. Drew has been developing and leading student movements of hundreds for 7+ years. He is a National Conference Speaker and Student Ministry Strategist who currently resides in Visalia, California with his wife of 3+ years Meagan. Drew's passion for student ministry comes from his desire to create and develop student ministries that not only are sustainable, but movements that see middle school & high school students of all ages reaching and influencing those around them.

CHAPTER TEN
Reimagining Your Children's Ministry Volunteers for Renewal
By Bill Hegedus

Have you ever had that panic-stricken moment when you're not sure you will have enough volunteers in the classrooms? Sunday's coming and so are the children, but you're not sure about the volunteers. This seems to be a common theme in children's ministry today. I would often think the verse "The harvest is plenty, but the workers are few" was written with the children's ministry in mind. When I started as a children's pastor, I felt this tension many times. I would do everything right on the front end, or so I thought. The schedule would have names listed in various spots and lesson plans would be emailed out, but inevitably every Friday and Saturday I would have several call outs. This drove me crazy. I was left wondering how can I get my volunteers to be consistent? Do I need to bribe them with doughnuts and coffee? I am not above a good bribe. I tried so many things but nothing fully worked. I read books, attended seminars and studied other strategies. Some things would work for a little while and others not at all. I couldn't wrap my head around it, why couldn't I get consistency in my volunteers. I needed some divine intervention. It's awesome how you can pray to God and He lets you know the answer was in front of you the whole time. He showed me that the problem was my mindset, how I viewed volunteers. I was viewing my job as a children's pastor to disciple children, which is true, and the volunteers are here a means for me do that, which is false. I realized I was having volunteers do ministry for me and not with me. I needed to reimagine the volunteers God gave me. I needed to view them through the lens of Christ. This caused me to think, If Jesus is our example for how to live a God honoring life, wouldn't He also be the best example of leadership there is. After all, the 12 men He led went on to change the world. I was just focused on getting volunteers placed in the rooms to make Sunday happen, but wasn't truly investing in them beyond just giving them the information and supplies they need to keep the kids safe and happy for an hour. I had fallen into the trap of volunteer placement instead of leadership development. Sadly, by doing this, I was allowing the tyranny of the urgent, Sunday's coming mentality, to sabotage the long term or future success of the children's ministry. The very children I care for are not getting the absolute best they deserve.

As I studied how Jesus led His disciples, three consistent themes jump out at me. I ended up calling them the 3 E's of leadership development. The best part is, that leadership development at its core is also discipleship. By doing these three things we saw discipleship happening on the team in a big way and also with the children we serve! Here are the three E's of leadership development and how we use them.

There is ENGAGE.

Jesus engaged the disciples right where they were and invited them directly to join him. Think of Peter at the boat and Matthew at his tax booth. Jesus personally invited them to follow Him. Jim Wideman, one of the gurus of children's ministry, stresses the importance of the personal ask. Not just asking someone to just help watch 2 year olds, but to be part of something that will change future lives. It's true, the best leaders I have were ones I asked directly.

That leads us to EQUIPPING.

When Jesus asked Peter to follow Him, He told Peter he was going to make him a fisher of men. He was going to equip him to accomplish something monumental. This is the biggest and most time-consuming step in the process. Jesus was equipping the disciples to carry the gospel to the world after He was gone. Not only that, but also how to equip others to do the same. So how do we apply this to children's ministry? First off, start by letting them know why children's ministry is so important and the difference they can make in the life of a child. The "why" always has to come before the "what" and the "how". Share stories of life change that has happened in the ministry. People are moved to action by inspiration not information. Then you can make a list of the 'what's' and the 'how's'. *What* to do in different situations and *how* to do certain tasks. How share the Gospel in an engaging way. And ultimately how to help build the team by engaging others and asking them to be a part of what God is doing in the lives of kids and families.

When I started in ministry I would only share the what and the how. I was unintentionally communicating to my volunteers that they where there to just accomplish tasks. Not very inspiring I know. That was where I was failing them. Thankfully, some of my biggest failures lead to breakthroughs.

That leads us to the final E: EMPOWERING.

After Jesus spent time equipping His disciples, He sent them out. He empowered them to do miracles and cast out demons. Sometimes they had success other times they failed. But Christ used these times of failure not to condemn, but to fine tune them. In ministry this can be one of the hardest things for us to do. Let go! I would often struggle with the mindset "if I wanted it done right I needed to do it myself." The more important the job was the more resistant I was to let it go. After all, I am the children's pastor. It is my job to make sure it gets done, right? Wrong! I forgot what my role is. It is to live out Ephesians 4:11-12. It's to EQUIP others to DO ministry so the church can be built up. You have to empower those you have equipped to do what you equipped them to do. They might not do it perfect the first time, but that's fine. It will allow you to help them become even better over time.

I have found the following 5 step process extremely helpful for implementing the three E's of leadership development. For this, let's use the example of equipping someone to be a small group leader for 1st graders.

The first step: they watch you do it. The best way to properly equip a team member is to show them the way you want it done by example. It is important to establish the standard you desire rather than to have them try and figure it out on their own. Don't just only hand them a check list or handbook and verbally describe the process. They will be more equipped if you also demonstrate how to do it as well. Have them watch as you explain what you are doing and why.

Practical Tools for Reinventing the Dying Church

Second step: do it together. Here you are inviting them to participate in leading. This will give them more of a feel of the role or task you are equipping them for. This is an important step not to skip. You don't want them to feel like they are being thrown to the wolves. Probably not a great way to put it, but when I have skipped this step that's exactly the kind of the look they would have on their face as I walk by the classroom. Remember they are partnering with you in ministry.

The third step: they do it while you watch. This gives them the true feeling of running the class but having the benefit having coaching immediately available. You have started the transition from equipping to empowering. This also gives the ability to fine tune any areas. Remember, you want them to be the best small group leader they can be. Don't rush this step and only move on to step four when you think they are ready.

The fourth step: do it on their own. Now you have given them complete ownership. By this step they should have complete confidence in their role. This also gives you the peace of mind that they are equipped to handle it on their own. Also, constantly remind them that they can come to you with any questions and you are always available to help. Before you know it, they will be ready to tackle the final step.

Step five: they find someone and repeat the steps 1-4 with them. Now that you have equipped and empowered them, have them go and engage other potential team members. The beauty of this is, now you have others helping build the team as well. By constantly doing this you will create a culture of leadership development. The hard part is that it takes time. So stick with it and you will be amazed at the results, just as I was.

Our role as a children's leader, or any leadership role for that matter, is to first pour into the lives of those we lead. Then our role should be to engage new people, equip them to be the best they can be, empower them to put what they learned into practice, and to be cheering them on the entire way. This is the heart of leadership development.

 Bill serves as the Family Pastor of the Bethlehem Church in Atlanta. He has over 15 year's experience ministering to kids and families. His heart and passion is to help kids understand and live out a personal relationship with Jesus Christ. Often described as a big kid himself, Bill uses laughter and innovation to do ministry in an exciting and memorable way kids enjoy.

CHAPTER ELEVEN
A Change of Heart:
The Role of Prayer in the Revitalization of the Church
By Chris Irving

Texans are fiercely independent. From the beginning of their fight for independence from Mexico in 1835 until now, no one tells a Texan what to do. The town in which I currently serve (Gonzales, Texas) is the epitome of Texas pride and independence. Our community flag is one that waves proudly and is known as the "Come and Take It" battle flag with its symbolic Lone Star and iconic cannon. The oppressive tyrant known as General Santa Anna forced the hand of the Texans, beginning the struggle for Texas independence right here in my hometown. The people wanted a change. The fight ensued and many lives were laid on the altar of freedom and independence. Texas changed for the better.

When the hand of a tyrant tried to selfishly force change, Santa Anna lost his empire. Let me suggest that you not try the Santa Anna method to bring about revitalization in your church. Instead, consider Sir Isaac Newton's first law of motion, which states "everything continues in a state of rest unless it is compelled to change by forces impressed upon it". While not a biblical principle, there is truth in this statement that applies to church revitalization.

Change begins in the heart and soul of the people. How do we, as leaders, change the hearts of men? Simply put, we cannot. But God can! Prayer is a vital component to revitalization because it is through prayer that God speaks to His people to impress the need for change. In an article in "Facts & Trends", Micah Fries lists 7 essentials for true church health. One of the seven is "prayerful dependence."[12] When, through prayer, we come to a place of total dependence upon God, revitalization can begin.

---

12 Fries, Micah. Facts & Trends. *"Say A-h-h-h: How to assess your church's well-being."* (Lifeway: Nashville, 2015). Volume 61. Number 3.

In Matthew 6:9-13, Jesus teaches us how to pray. The disciple's prayer serves as a model prayer that we can employ for heart-change, which ultimately leads to revitalized churches. When we pray the Jesus-way, our hearts adjust to His by dwelling in community with Him, our vision and priorities conform to His and we come to depend upon God for His provision of daily needs, forgiveness, and leadership.

OUR HEART CONFORMS TO HIS

Have you ever noticed when you're driving in your car and there appears, over time, a slight vibration in your tires? The calibration in the balance of the tires is out of sync, causing the vibration of the car.

In the same way that a vehicle's tires require calibration, we too need to have our hearts calibrated to God's. When we pray, "Our Father in heaven," we acknowledge our relationship to Him and His position of authority over us. He is our Father first and He is in heaven on His sovereign throne, in complete control of creation and His kingdom. The truth of who He is and where He is causes our hearts to shift.

The need for revitalization is not always noticeable right away, but like the tire that gradually shifts out of balance, the local church can slip into a place in which revitalization is required. The adjustment must be made as we seek God the Father. The Fatherhood of God ought to settle uncertainties and give hope as the church prays for revitalization.

Change happens as we conform to His will. God's name, purpose, and priority are most hallowed when the church behaves in conformity to His will. David said it right in Psalm 16:8 when he wrote, "I have set the LORD continually before me."

OUR VISION CONFORMS TO HIS

Sometimes, the ride of a car is turbulent because the wheels are not aligned correctly. Because the wheels are out of alignment, the tires wear unevenly, leading to other serious problems. Our vision can get out of alignment with God's kingdom purposes. God's vision for the church is found in the prayer of Jesus. As we pray for the Kingdom of God to come, the vision of the church changes as His kingdom transforms our hearts into kingdom-centered Jesus-followers.

I love the way The Message states Proverbs 29:18, *"If people can't see what God is doing, they stumble all over themselves; But when they attend to what He reveals, they are most blessed."* As we pray for His kingdom to come and for the accomplishing of God's will, our vision should naturally conform to His. If this conformity does not happen in the hearts of the people, any outward change will be short-lived. As the church prays this truth, the vision of the people will begin to conform to God's kingdom vision and the church will become relevant and vital. How can we see what God is doing if we are not spending time in prayer?

Should we continue to pray for our focus to be on evangelism, discipleship and all the other stuff that goes with church life or should we pray for the Kingdom of God to come? To live and pray the Kingdom of God is not a prayer to be prayed in addition to all the other stuff…it *is* the stuff. Discipleship, fellowship, evangelism, ministry and worship don't happen outside the kingdom; those things *are* the Kingdom.

OUR NEEDS ARE MET TO FULFILL HIS PURPOSE

In order to thrive and drive, your car has certain needs. Routine maintenance is a must for any car, no matter the make or model of the vehicle. As you journey the road of revitalization, you'll learn to depend on God more and more to meet your needs. This is like God saying, "Hey, I've got your back." God will provide all of the church's needs according to His glorious riches in Christ Jesus.

Look at what God does for His people while they journey through the desert, leaving Egypt. They are in His will, traveling to the Promised Land and each day He provides manna for them. The "daily bread" they need in order to thrive in their journey falls from heaven each morning.

We need God's daily provision, but we also need forgiveness from God and to dispense this same forgiveness to others in the church. No doubt you will face opposition to the revitalization adjustments needing to be made. But you cannot harbor the bitterness that naturally comes because bitterness is dangerous poison to the heart of the revitalizer. You too must forgive.

Finally, we need God's leadership, protection, and deliverance. As you pray for His leadership, protection from temptation leading to failure and for deliverance, God's providence is evident and His glory is on display. This, after all, is the purpose of the church…to make God known to the nations.

You cannot force change any more than I can force a square peg into a round hole, but you can intentionally begin a journey of prayer focused on changing the hearts of the people you serve, thus changing the heart of the church. The result is a healthy and vital church. After all, prayer changes people. And who knows but that the heart changed most might just be yours.

Chris has served in ministry for 15 years in Texas. He led a small rural church to revitalization and is currently involved in the revitalization process of First Baptist Gonzales. He earned his Masters of Divinity at Southwestern Baptist Theological Seminary and his Doctorate of Ministry in leadership studies at Midwestern Baptist Theological Seminary. Dr. Irving aims to help pastors equip the lay leadership of the church to serve in ministry. He and his wife, Amber have been married for 14 years and have six children.

CHAPTER TWELVE
The Pastor's Personal Life and Leadership Capacity
By Greg Kappas

Leadership trumps preaching! I have sat with many pastors who are dynamic preachers as they look me in the eye with concern and exhaustion. "Greg, I have prayed and preached my heart out...people respond to the messages but I just do not see them staying at our church. We cannot keep them. I know it is all about the Kingdom, but we cannot keep them here."

In church revitalization, the sooner you grasp that leadership development is as important or even more important than preaching and teaching, you will have turned a corner toward church health. To establish healthy leaders in your church, things begin with Jesus and you. Do not train leaders to multiply leaders if you are not doing the same!

Where do we begin?

It all starts with a paradigm that initiates with 4 Phases: **Reaching New People** is the first circle and continues in that setting while living out these other 3 leadership truths. Training new converts, emerging leaders, new leaders and established leaders in a process of the second circle **Training in the Basics** of Christianity. As we **Train in the Basics**, we continue to live out the first circle **Reach New People**.
As we continue to **Reach New People** and **Train them in the Basics** of Christianity, we then move to the third circle **Equip to Serve**. We equip these leaders to serve Jesus Christ in light of their passions and gift mix. Finally we then **Keep Reaching New People**, while we then move them into **Training in the Basics** of the faith, **Equipping them to Serve** and then the fourth circle **Mobilizing these leaders for Ministry.**

Scores of pastoral leaders have stated to me that they are not gifted in evangelism and therefore they seek to hire or find a key leader who can do the work of an evangelist and even fulfill the function of an evangelist as in Ephesians 4. That misses the point. Finding someone with a gift mix to complement your own endowment from the Lord never is an excuse for personally avoiding opportunities to reach out to unbelievers and believers who are not worshipping Jesus.

If we do not model **Reaching New People** in our own personal lives, we have limited our capacity of leadership and most importantly quelled the work of the Holy Spirit personally. Pulpit illustrations dating back 5 years when you last saw someone come to Jesus personally in your interaction is weak if not diluted at best. Looking at your pulpit ministry as the only way to do evangelism is simply cowardly. Praise God for the people who come to Jesus through your preaching and teaching ministry, but they can also be won to Christ by you at Starbucks, at Panera, and going to a movie theatre to relate to culture. Saturate yourself with the Biblical motif to **Reach New People**.

Remember, reaching the lost and those not walking with Christ fulfills your ministry. "As for you, always be sober minded, endure suffering, do the work of an evangelist, fulfill your ministry." 2 Timothy 4:5 Once people come to Jesus and are now regenerated, they cannot stay there of course. In fact, my long-time mentor, Dr. Earl D. Radmacher who went to be with our Lord on December 8th of 2014 often stated "The Christian army has spiritual babes that need to be transitioned from infancy to the infantry." We are in a spiritual war and we need to move these youngsters into soldiers.

While the movement takes place to **Train these new people in the Basics**, none of us can lose the passion to be obedient to **Reach New People**. Fresh lakes stay healthy with new water.
Training in the Basics focuses on matters such as assurance of salvation, learning to share your faith, prayer, Bible study, fasting, the Spirit and Word controlled life, Scripture memorization, etc. These are the foundational matters to help people be stabilized and progress in the Lord. Great ministries like the Navigators, Inter-Varsity, CRU all still focus on helping people move forward in the elementary processes of their faith in Jesus Christ.

Practical Tools for Reinventing the Dying Church

As a pastoral leader, if you do not help these new people become established in their faith, then you are shaking their hands as they walk into corporate worship, giving them a baby bottle of milk as they come in, and burping the babies as they leave. Think and pray about this…without initial pouring of spiritual concrete, we just keep the new person vulnerable and placed in shifting sand.

As these new believers and defeated Christians see their lives turned around through being **Trained in the Basics,** they keep focusing on **Reaching New People** as they grow in Christ. True discipleship and leadership understands there is no full growth without reaching the lost and those who are not moving forward spiritually. These new people also move forward in Christ through a few months of **Training in the Basics.** Be sure to keep this process somewhat short as these new people need to be **Equipped to Serve**. Hebrews 6 encourages us to move on in our faith.

People need to know what their spiritual gifts are and how to use them. As followers of Christ we must know what our natural gifts and talents are as they also come from the Lord. This is a crucial step in **Equipped to Serve**. When people are equipped for the ministry God has for them, they are passionate and motivated about making a difference for the King and His Kingdom. Along with our spiritual gifts and talents, we need to understand the needs around us and beyond.

What are our eternal purposes as believers and how has God wired you to fulfill those purposes? What is your uniqueness and contribution to the Body of Christ? What are your spiritual passions? What is your calling? How has God shaped you for eternal impact?

The finest ministry and resources that I know of in the world in this realm, center with Kingdom Mobilization. Visit kingmo.org and see what Pastor Nolen Rollins and his team have developed for you and your people. Simply fantastic! How can we read Ephesians 4 and not want to connect with a process like this? After our conversion to Christ and grasping the Spirit and Word controlled life, it seems to me that God's endowment in our lives, through spiritual gifts and our natural gifts may be the most important truths that we can absorb in life.

Being **Mobilized for Ministry** releases the joy of how we are so important to the Lord and His Kingdom purposes. Where does He want us? Are we serving Him here in this same city or town, and the same church? Are we called to serve Him in another location with a dynamic church? Are we called to serve Him in the same church here but also touch other locations through technology? Where in the world does the Lord want us?

This process of leadership development deals with releasing and deploying. Wherever the Christian soldier goes, he or she focuses on fulfilling the God ordained wiring that Jesus has placed in them. As they discover this wiring, they serve Christ in their strengths and also keep **Reaching New People** in the process.

This is why leadership development trumps preaching! Disciples who make disciples who make disciples, leads to leaders who make leaders who make leaders for Jesus.

Dr. Greg Kappas has been an integral part of The Timothy Initiative (TTI) leadership team over the past seven years. He's served in many capacities as TTI Vice President, church planting training guru, curriculum development and our resident theologian. Greg is also the President and Founder of Grace Global Network. He is an incredible servant leader, ministry coach and friend to many. Kappas is a frequent writer for the Church Revitalizer magazine and has coached ministers on five continents.

CHAPTER THIRTEEN
Desire for Authenticity Not Cultural Relevancy
By Jim Grant

In, this chapter, I will try to investigate whether Church Revitalization is relevant. Is there a need for Church Revitalization; in other words, does the church stand in need of restoration and renewal? Are the modern church formats that lead to increased attendance numbers but little discipleship really making a Kingdom difference? I would hope that you would already be familiar with the cultured Christianity we face today in many churches and denominations. The church and culture are at odds, not that this should surprise us. In the recent decisions of the SCOTUS, it is very obvious that American culture is out of sync with biblical Christianity and Scripture. There has been a great outcry from many Christian key leaders. The cultural wars have been going on for decades. The struggle for effective evangelization of the Gospel has been confronted with the struggle of becoming more like the "culture trying to be reached" versus "being stalwart against culture." There have been many moves towards trying to make worship and church environments amicable towards the lost. The thought is that if "we look like them, we'll be able to connect with them." The struggle that occurs with changes of worship and practices, however, is that we may engage the culture, but lose our relevancy. The statistics quoted by the researchers indicate that the church is in trouble – decline-plateaued and dying.

As a revitalization pastor, I am compelled to look at the situation of the church and compare it not to statistics, but to the Word of God. How does the church compare to what Jesus said that He would build? Should the church look more like the culture in which it is located? Should the church compromise on dress, music, facilities and the like to accommodate [draw interests from] the unchurched? That is the greatest question facing any local or regional church. If a church accommodates the desires of the "world" will it still be relevant? The answer is multifaceted. The word relevant means effective, pertinent and applicable. While this doesn't of itself give the answer, it does make us think of our goals and results. There is a position many, many churches have taken that theorize that it doesn't matter what the process is, as long as the desired result is achieved. Again we are confronted with the question, *"What is the church trying to do?"*. If the goal is to gain more people in attendance, many things will draw a crowd, but seldom does the crowd stay long after the event.

The church is not winning the younger generations to the Gospel. There may be mega churches with thousands of attendees, but what is the effect on the surrounding community. We have been called to be light in darkness, salt to the world and be in the world but not of it. We live here, but we are not to be overtaken by the things of the world. There must be a definitive difference between the world and Christianity. If there is no difference - if we look like, talk like and act like the world, are we relevant? I think that there must be an engaging of the culture around us, but if we have become so visually and functionally like the world, then the world makes the decision that "the church" is no longer relevant. *Here is the key point – the world determines if the church is relevant to them, not by agreement with them, but in contrast to them.*

In America we have organizations that fight each other on both sides of a moral or ethical issue. While the advocate for each side of the issue provides great commentary and social media buzz, rarely does it provide a platform for resolving the issue. The truth of the matter is that there should be great contrast between what the world believes and practices versus what the church believes and practices. The reality is this: *"The world culture is better at living out who they are, than the believing church being who they are supposed to be"*. There is great need to engage the cultural issues facing us today. However, engaging the issues has to be more than rhetoric. The greatest change agent in changing the world and its immoral ways is showing the lost the love of the Lord. Argument doesn't change views and lives, but the love of Christ poured out of the believing community into the hurting unsaved community can.

If the church decline and death problems are to be addressed, the purpose of the church must be restored. We have been sent to make disciples, teaching them whatever Jesus taught. Ed Stetzer identified three kinds of Christians: cultural,

Practical Tools for Reinventing the Dying Church

congregational or committed. There is one more type of Christian – carnal. The Church is struggling, and in our struggles we cannot become more like the world; we must become more like Jesus. Therein is the relevancy. Churches decline and die because they forgot their mission. Two problems exist; first is the staunch position of isolation of the church from anything that is viewed as a threat to the past. This usually results in a rapidly dying congregation. The second problem is cultured Christianity, and its loss of relevancy. Both situations call for restoration and renewal. The older generations cannot be closed minded towards the changes of community and culture. The cultural Christians cannot become so like the culture that they lose ability to "save out of the world." There must be a return back to the mission of the church. When the church remembers and returns to the people of God, and lives out visibly in the culture, God will change the community. Countless times, Israel drifted into "name only people of God;" having allowed the culture to invade and takeover. Solomon is a classic example of how cultural acceptance can infiltrate and draw the people of God away from the Lord. Israel was chosen by God to be the witness of God in the world. He cautioned Israel over and over – do not become like the people in the land. In modern day application, if the church is going to be relevant, there must be a difference between believers and the world. Relevant – again means effective, pertinent and applicable; authentic. The world is tired of plastic; they desire the REAL world and if the church is viewed as the plastic world where they already live, well, then the church just lost its relevancy to them.

Jim Grant Serves as the Lead Pastor of Heartland Baptist Church in Alton, Illinois. He is a veteran with 25 years of service in the Air Force. His extensive travels, while in the military, allowed him the unique ability to have served in the full spectrum of churches, styles, and health. He has a M.Div. with Biblical Languages from Southwestern Baptist Theological Seminary, and a D.Min. from Midwestern Baptist Theological Seminary with a concentration on Church Revitalization. Jim is a frequent contributor to the Church Revitalizer Magazine and a regular presenter at the Renovate

National Church Revitalization Conference. He has been married to his wife for 39 years and they have two daughters and four grandchildren.

CHAPTER FOURTEEN
The Greatest Challenge in Revitalization
By John Kimball

I've been a turn-around pastor. I've personally ministered in both rural and suburban settings. My experience is also national, working with local churches in virtually every region of the United States. There are many things I would tell you are non-negotiable if your church is to experience true revitalization. But there is one factor that, if missing, will prevent all revitalization efforts from ever taking root. And it has absolutely nothing to do with your pastor, your strategy or the demographics within which you must minister.

When a local church determines that it is in plateau or decline, there are many options it will typically pursue: seek out resources or seminars on growth, find or develop new programs, appoint new leadership (sometimes including the pastor), among others. But in most cases, such pursuits will not quell the hemorrhaging, let alone bring the church out of its nosedive. This is because the problem is most often systemic within the congregation itself.

In over 25 years of ministry, I have yet to find a church that is experiencing revitalization problems where systemic issues were not in the driver's seat. The challenge is helping the congregation to see that they must change if their church is to return to fruitful kingdom ministry. Here's the bottom line: Church Revitalization is only possible when the congregation is willing to directly engage in disciple-making.

Yes, the pastor must preach in a way that speaks directly to the hearts of those the church is called to reach. Yes, some form of small group ministry is mandatory if the quality of relationships required to grow are going to form in the church family. Yes, intercessory prayer must be powerful and consistent in the life of the church. All these are true and more. However, none of these qualities will be able to turn around a church whose congregation has quietly and collectively stopped living out the Great Commission on a personal level.

I understand that many churches are into their second or even third generation of members who have not actively participated in discipling people in Christ. I have faced the push back of those who have lived most of their lives with "discipleship" defined as "teaching people about Jesus and the Bible." But it is mandatory that we rediscover the New Testament truth that discipleship is not so much about *information* as it is about *transformation!* And there are way too many people in churches all across America who *know* a lot about Jesus and the Bible, but whose lives look no different than the world. Churches are filled today with people who were "saved" years ago, but who are still nearly as spiritually immature as the day they called Jesus "Lord." This has to change.

Discipleship is not a class. It's not a 13-week study. It's not what you hire the pastor to do. Discipleship is a life-on-life investment into a few key others guiding them to demonstrate spiritual growth, maturity and fruit in their walk with Jesus. Discipleship is something that every member of the congregation must actively do – and it is something that every member of the congregation must also actively receive. From the youngest to the oldest believer, we never stop becoming more like King Jesus until we stand before Him in glory.

In some shape or form, I have often been told, "Well, preacher, that's not the way we define 'church' around here." I understand. But at some point, church members need to recognize and accept their own part in their church's decline. Our Jesus commissioned us all to make disciples – and until that once again becomes our primary activity, local churches will continue to wane.

It's not easy, but it is possible for the church that wants to honor Jesus. It may require some outside help at first, but as the church's leadership begins to disciple people – and they do so with a 2 Timothy 2:2 spirit where we disciple people to disciple people to disciple people – it is utterly amazing what can happen in the life and ministry of a local church. It's not a magic bullet. It's just simple obedience to the Great Commission on the personal level.

Practical Tools for Reinventing the Dying Church

So, what about your congregation? How many books have you read on church revitalization? How many seminars have you attended? How many assessments or demographic studies have you done? All of these are great tools, but unless they lead us to effectively address the systemic problem, they will remain fruitless. Is your congregation – the people who sit in your pews on Sunday – ready to take an active role in discipleship? Will they become willing partners with the Holy Spirit in leading others to maturity? Will they, at every age, humbly allow other believers to pour into their lives so that they too may experience growth, fruit and an even deeper walk with Jesus.

Dr. John Kimball is Director of Church Development for the Conservative Congregational Christian Conference. He has nearly 30 years of pastoral experience, most of it in revitalization ministry, and coaches pastors and churches through development in his denomination and in partnership with the Praxis Center for Church Development. John serves as the Lead Pastor/Planter of Palmwood Church in Metropolitan Orlando.

CHAPTER FIFTEEN
Tribal Leadership and Church Revitalization
By Kenneth Priest

Much is presently being written on the topic of church revitalization. Many speakers and writers are addressing the crisis issues that churches are facing. However, what about the rest of the churches in need of revitalization? The ones who are not in crisis situations; typically seen as the plateauing churches; but some of the declining churches as well.

Most revitalization experts agree it takes 1000 days, or three years, to turn around a church. In some scenarios, there is not enough time to go slow…but what if there were? What is the ideal revitalization strategy shift in a church that has a life expectancy of four, five, or even more years left? What should a leader do?

My opinion, this is where tribal leadership comes in. Understand, this is not a new concept. This terminology may not have been used in the past, but the philosophy has. The thesis idea is this; become a part of the tribe before trying to do too much. Simple right?! Until you are in the scenario.

Most revitalizers are high capacity leaders. They are not satisfied with the status quo, especially when the status quo is not engaging the community for the cause of Christ. So what should a leader do that has time and wants to rightly effect change and not lose the "shareholders". (*Shareholder* is an affectionate term I use to describe the persons in the church who are essentially bankrolling the ministry. Too often these are the ones who immediately get marginalized during a change of pastoral leadership; and pastors get frustrated when they leave and the budget is no longer there to support the ministry. Often, pastors even accuse these persons of being spiritually immature for leaving and are critical, when the reality is that the pastor did not involve them in the decision making and truly lead as a servant leader being the under-shepherd God intended for the pastor to be).

Practical Tools for Reinventing the Dying Church

Tribal leadership is the art of joining the tribe in order to bring about change without losing those presently engaged and involved in ministry…this is tough, but needed.

The difficulty of becoming a part of the tribe is, it takes time. This is why you cannot use this method in a crisis situation, but where time permits, use it to your advantage. Join the tribe, become the pastor they talk about and love and then begin to offer recommendations for change. You will use your honeymoon phase to initiate a couple of immediate, necessary strategy shifts; but save your big capital for when they have accepted you as part of them. No one can tell you exactly when this happens; but philosophically, this is when they want you doing the weddings and funerals, and not the previous pastor. This can take upwards of three or more years to achieve. But when it does, you are the pastor and leader of the tribe.

Step One

Learn who the influencers are, both positive and negative (in these longer revitalization scenarios, they are typically both present). Whether a matriarch or patriarch; church treasurer or deacon, make certain you get to know these persons and their circles of influence. The hidden relationships are often the ones causing the most issues for pastors. As a pastor, you should know whom all influencers are connected to before you make any decisions. When dealing with a positive influencer, if the person is on your side…you just got buy-in from the majority. Likewise, the same is true for your negative influencer…you can will have an uphill battle without buy-in here.

Step Two

Learn your personal leadership style…and adjust when necessary. Fox example, I have a personality that is a high director and high analytical. This means I make decisions quickly based on data I have assessed and make judgments based on performance. If a ministry is showing success, my leadership style leans toward focusing attention in this area because it is performing well. The problem with this model, other areas might get neglected, simply because I have evaluated a success driven through performance…in this scenario, some of my shareholders might get left on the sidelines, feel marginalized and ultimately leave the church. A revitalizer must know his tendencies and strive to overcome them. Certainly, in a crisis scenario, a high director/analytical leader will do great. However, in these longer time revitalization scenarios, it might be best if I adjust my style; move out of my core and rely on God to use me to focus on functioning more as an inspirational leader to motivate the weaker areas to have similar impact or more on the analytical to determine why we are having more of an impact in one area over another. The life lesson here is, do not go around with the attitude of "this is how I am, and others need to adjust to me" but rather, demonstrate the leadership styles of Christ and lead for the given situation you are in as a servant leader.

Step Three

Know your demographics. Not just of the community, but of the church. Understand who your people are and who you need to reach. Example: I once was working in a revitalization situation as a consultant. In meeting with the pastor, I learned, like many of us, he was a creature of habit. He came and left church the exact same way every day he was there. Why?! Because they were just off the exit of a major interstate. That was the fastest way to go; why take backstreets? In accepting my challenge to "know your demographics" (one of my exercises to have the pastor and church leaders go on a prayer walk around the church neighborhoods), the pastor learned who his church was, and who they were not reaching. Namely the Vietnamese community which was two blocks behind the church. This was an eye-opening experience for him.

Step Four

I do not want to under or overstate this, but develop a plan. Strategies are not wrong. Planning is not wrong. Look at creation; God's plan is intricate and specific. Man, could not be created on the first day since there was no place for him. Pastors and churches need plans for reaching their communities. Determine who needs to be reached (from step three) and develop a plan

Step Five

Execute the plan. Churches that are succeeding in church revitalization are actually doing what they set out to do. This is the Great Commission; Jesus set us on a strategy to engage the nations for his cause from the beginning…and that is simply what we need to do.

Kenneth Priest serves as the Director of Convention Strategies for the Southern Baptists of Texas Convention. He holds a Doctor of Educational Ministry degree with an emphasis in Church Revitalization from Midwestern Baptist Theological Seminary, Kansas City, MO.

Chapter SIXTEEN
Running with Tortoises
By Rob Hurtgen

. . . let us run with endurance the race that lies before us, keeping our eyes on Jesus, the source and perfecter of our faith, . . ." Hebrews 12:1b – 2a

> *"Slow and steady does it every time!"*
> Tortoise to Hare, *Aesop's Fables*

The classic children's story *The Tortoise and the Hare* has been told and retold numerous times. No matter how many times the story varies in every race the slow, steady and consistent Tortoise beats the impetuous and attention deficit disordered Hare. Slow and steady endurance wins the race.

Like the Tortoise, church revitalizers must also learn to practice steady endurance to see vibrancy return to a church whose pulse is weak. While there are instances that demand quick solutions, I contend that the majority of churches in need of revitalization need slow, steady, focused and consistent leadership to return to health and vibrancy. Revitalizers – those who, by God's grace, intentionally work to see restoration of biblical health to a church – must not only possess the conviction of what the church should be paired with a unique vision for the local church, they must also develop, practice and maintain a consistent approach on the path to renewal. Like the tortoise, revitalizers must keep the vision of the finish line in view with every enduring step they take.

Getting Lost in The Moment

The necessary endurance is derailed more often not by discouragement but by getting lost in the urgency of the moment. To endure means that there is something worth enduring for. Something that will cause strain, trial, suffering and hardships that must be pushed through for a greater reward. The reason many do not endure is not because of the price demanded from them but because the urgency of the immediate is blinding to the future that God has instore. Revitalizers are in great danger if they only see the immediate void of faith in the future. The Bible has several examples of those for whom the urgency of the immediate blinded them to what God could do in and through them for his glory.

While Gideon was threshing wheat in a cave, hiding from the Midianites an angel of the Lord came to him saying, "The Lord is with you, mighty warrior." Nothing about this moment in Gideon's life revealed that the Lord was with him, he was mighty or even a warrior. God, however, saw what he was going to do through Gideon. In that moment, all Gideon could see was the dust from the wheat.

Samson was a judge that paralleled his time. His preconception calling was clear. An angel of the Lord gave specific details of the Nazarite vow that he was to be bound by. Yet Samson regularly neglected his vow focusing only the immediate losing sight of what God wanted to accomplish through him. It was not until he was blinded and, by God's grace, his "hair began to grow" did Samson truly see.

Sarah laughed when she overheard three men speaking, telling Abraham that this time next year she would have a son. All she saw was an old, shriveled woman with an unused and unusable womb. Cobwebs where conception should be. She saw the immediate when God was delivering on the promise.

Revitalizers must lead with the biblical conviction as to who the church should be while not getting lost in the overwhelming tyranny of the immediate. Revitalizers must call on the church they serve to trust in the Lord who is able to do far more abundantly than all that we ask or think, according to the power at work within us (Eph. 3:20). Spiritual endurance is built when we despite the urgency of the immediate, pray and work and work and pray. When we have worked and prayed, then we pray and work. Revitalizers must trust the Lord in what he is doing and what he wants to accomplish regardless of the tyranny of the immediate.
I'll never forget the conversation with a new Youth Pastor. He was excited about pursuing God's calling in ministry and finally starting in his first church. Within a couple of months though he found himself frustrated. He wanted to know why weren't the

students responding? How could they still be missing the last youth pastor? Didn't they care about God or the lost at all? Three months into his first ministry he thought he was a failure and was ready to quit. Maybe he misunderstood God's calling? Maybe he was just in the wrong place?

Fortunately, I was able to pass on to him the same counsel that was passed on to me. I am certain this same counsel was handed down to the pastor who passed it to me; ministry is a marathon, not a sprint. Ministry requires endurance.

Marathoners train for endurance. A typical training schedule for the average weekend warrior marathoner is to build each weeks training on the previous week. If you ran five miles this week, next week run six, and on and on until the goal of running 26.2 miles seems reachable. This progressive preparation trains the muscles to know how to endure for the four, five and even longer hours of running. Sprinters on the other hand train for quick and explosive reaction. Their physiology develops different than a marathoner. For sprinters, their race is over before the marathoner has even found their stride. Building a lifelong ministry of renewal requires the revitalizer learn to build endurance.

Learning to endure presses back against the tyranny of the immediate. Instead of getting lost in the urgent, the revitalizer who learns to endure knows where the church is heading and are confident when the bumps come they too will pass. The pulse of the church did not weaken quickly. It will not be renewed quickly. Health is pressed towards step-by-step, stride-by-stride. One eye on where they are going, another on where they are.

The Bible Calls for Endurance

Fortunately endurance is not a genetic trait. The Bible teaches and encourages believers to endure meaning then that endurance is a learnable trait. In Galatians 6:9 Paul tells the Galatian church to not grow weary in doing good. The only reason to tell someone to not grow weary in doing good is because doing good day after day, week after week, year after

Practical Tools for Reinventing the Dying Church

year, uncertain if any good will come of the work, will wear you out. Endurance is built when even exhausted you do not wear out. In Philippians Paul encourages the church to build endurance by pressing on (Phil. 3:14). Again, one only needs to be reminded to press on if there is a hint of giving up. You can hear the sense of contentment and satisfaction dripping from the pages when Paul tells Timothy, "I fought the good fight, I have finished the race, I have kept the faith." Press on. Diligently, steadily with endurance, press on. The scriptures call for normal, every day, endurance.

Learning to Endure

Revitalizers must learn the endurance necessary to see, by God's grace, renewal comes to the church they serve. Stepping daily towards health and vitality requires practicing some critical daily disciplines. While there are many principles, practices and models available for renewal there are some critical issues that must be addressed to learn endurance.

Don't Neglect Your Soul

First, regularly practice your own spiritual disciplines. "The Spiritual Disciplines are those personal and corporate disciplines that promote spiritual growth. They are the habits of devotion and experiential Christianity that have been practiced by the people of God since biblical times."[13] Those personal and intimate times of scripture reading, prayer, memorization, Sabbath and other practices will become both an anchor and armor in the work of renewal.

To some a warning to not neglect the personal practices of spiritual disciplines may seem minor, trite even. However, to neglect these personal spiritual practices is the quickest route to personal implosion. When we begin to lose our awe of God, not only do we lose our spirituality but our sense of what it means to

---

13 Donald Whitney, *Spiritual Disciplines For The Christian Life*, (Colorado Springs, Colorado: NavPress, 1991), 17.

be created in the image of God.[14] Without an awe of God, we have returned by our own neglect, to making bricks without straw.

Each revitalizer must remember that intentionally working towards spiritual renewal where sickness dwells is to engage in a spiritual battle. The enemy does not easily give back ground that he has claimed. There will be issues emerge that you did not even know about. Discouragement will be a river that will run deep and often. Revitalizers must show up daily and deeply rooted in the awe of God.

Include in your ministry labors the discipline of Sabbath. In ministry in general and Church Revitalization specific there is always something that needs to be done. The gospel needs to be shared. There is a bible study that needs to be taught. A committee meeting that needs leadership. A disenfranchised church member that, even though they have not been to the church in ten years, must simply speak to the pastor now. The list of demands can seem endless.

The Sabbath is essential to remember in whose image we were created and in whose ownership we rest. Create a specific time in your calendar to rest and to reconnect with your spouse and children. To remember what it means to just be you. Rest is essential to building spiritual endurance.

Show Up for Work

Secondly, show up for work. Paul reminds Timothy in his second and most personal letter to "do the work of an evangelist, fulfill your ministry." (2 Tim. 4:5). So much speculation has been written as to why Timothy needed this reminder. Perhaps he possessed a timid nature. Maybe his

---

14 For an excellent and much more articulate expression of the loss of spirituality and humanity listen to Paul Tripp, *Dangerous Calling: A Workshop with Paul Tripp,* The Gospel Coalition Conference, April 9, 2013, https://www.thegospelcoalition.org/article/a-dangerous-calling.

physical ailments caused him to shrink back from work of the ministry. Perhaps he simply needed a reminder to show up for work. We may never have a clear agreement as to why this reminder was needed but most will agree this reminder is still needed. Do the work of an evangelist, fulfill your ministry.

Cal Ripken Jr. has received numerous accolades throughout his baseball career. He is perhaps most known for his record of playing 2,632 consecutive games earning him the title of the "Iron Man" of baseball. Ripken has been quoted in numerous sources, and most particularly in the prelude of his 2007 book *Get in the Game,* as to what it takes to play every day. He writes, "I didn't just show up for work, as has sometimes been said. I also showed up to work."[15] That sharp distinctive between showing up *for* work and showing up *to* work is subtle but huge.

To show up for work is to simply be there. To show up to work is being prepared to get things done. Church revitalization is a ministry that requires more than just showing up. Church revitalization demands showing up to work. Endurance is built especially when we do not want to practice endurance.

In the ministry of church revitalization, there will be days when you do not want to show up let alone show up for work. There will be days when you will think that being a funeral director to bury the dead would be better than being in a ministry to raise the dead. These are the days to show up for the calling that God has placed within you. Revitalizers must possess the internal resolve to show up every day for work.

Build 90-Day Goals

---

15 Don Yaeger, "Lessons from Sports: Call Ripken Jr." *Success,* March 15, 2009, http://www.success.com/article/lessons-from-sports-cal-ripken-jr.

Third, clearly write out the goals the Lord has put in your heart. Embrace the permission to dream of what big, holy and audacious things God could do through your life and in your church. The best step you can take with those big things you are asking the Lord for – and I wish I had known this twenty years ago – is to translate those large goals into 90-day goals.

Every 90 days with prayer, seeking great wisdom and perhaps counsel, evaluate what needs to be done in the next 90 days to continue to move towards health. Endurance is fostered when progress made in small amounts towards renewal can be seen. By only looking at the bigger goals and ignoring the regular update the revitalizer is creating a path towards discouragement.

Avoid the temptation to only limit 90-day goals to the work church revitalization. Evaluate every area of your life. Both the roles that have been ordained by God – self, spouse, parent, child – and the roles you have embraced such as pastor, revitalizer, and pewee baseball coach.[16] Clarify what needs to be done in the next 90-days to move towards these bigger goals.

Reducing your large goals into 90-day goals will not only help clarify and direct what needs to be done weekly and even daily towards renewal it also pushes back discouragement. A big goal may not have been reached but more was done than if nothing had been done. Progress has been made. Isaiah 32:8 says, "He who is noble plans noble things, and on noble things he stands." "In other words, making plans for good makes a difference."[17]

Compassionately Communicate Early and Often

---

16 For greater reading on the subject of roles please see C.J. Mahaney's work entitled *Biblical Productivity* at http://www.cjmahaney.com/wp-content/uploads/2016/01/Biblical-Productivity.pdf and Matthew Perman's work *What's Best Next: How the Gospel Transforms the Way You Get Things Done.*

17 Perman, Matthew Aaron (2014-03-04). What's Best Next: How the Gospel Transforms the Way You Get Things Done (p. 261). Zondervan. Kindle Edition.

Practical Tools for Reinventing the Dying Church

Fourth, compassionately communicate early and often. As a revitalizer, you are working with an existing church whose pulse is weak. A church that is not healthy often acts like patients who are not healthy. If you take three different people and give them the exact diagnosis one may deny the diagnosis, another receive it but may refuse to do anything about it, while the third will receive the diagnosis and aggressively act to combat the illness. Members of an unhealthy church will act the same way.

The *deniers* of the congregation will insist that there is no problem. The *unwilling* see the problems but cannot bring themselves to do anything about the problem. The *ambitious* saw the issues months ago and are willing to do whatever they need to do to address the problem. Do not be surprised when the *deniers* conflict with the *ambitious* and both become frustrated with each other adding to the conflict that may have already existed. As the revitalization pastor, you get to speak to all three.

Communicate early and often. If you do not know the answer, find out. If you've made a mistake, confess it. It is critical to compassionately communicate clearly and often. Plan to have the same conversation several times. Communication breeds confidence. Confidence may be the only equity your revitalization work has.

Learning Endurance is Critical

I can say that these are four critical tools for revitalizing the dying church because I have violated every one of them in my own work of revitalization. Each time I have ignored these four critical areas I have become frustrated, discouraged and contributed to the sickness of the church rather than leading towards health. and steady with endurance does it every time.

Rob Hurtgen is the Senior Pastor of First Baptist Church Chillicothe, Missouri. He is completing a D.Min from Midwestern Baptist Theological Seminary and is a contributor to a variety of blogs, magazines and journals. He and his wife Shawn have been married since 1995 and have five children.

CHAPTER SEVENTEEN
Pitfalls of Revitalizers
By Michael Atherton

Have you ever attempted to assemble something for which you did not have the directions? I am thinking about a swing set…who would want to have to put a swing set together without the directions? Clearly, there are obvious problems when trying to accomplish a task for which there is ambiguity on one hand or outright chaos on the other. Such is the case for revitalization. What is church revitalization? Who is to lead church revitalization? How is church revitalization to be done? All of these questions (and many more) are very legitimate questions and yet the lack of answers can make us feel like we are trying to put together a swing set with no directions. In this article, I am going to share some thoughts as it relates leading revitalization; specifically identifying some pitfalls that you will want to avoid as a revitalizer.

It seems reasonable at this juncture to help define what we are talking about when we talk about Revitalization. Church revitalization is the *process in which a church is renewed in their determination to experience healthy and sustained spiritual, numerical, and organizational growth by refocusing on their God-given mission as expressed through their obedience to Scripture.* In my life, our church experienced revitalization when God led Cornerstone Baptist Church and University Hills Baptist Church to merge together in 2008. Though both churches were relatively healthy churches, both churches were aware that they were not meeting their potential, due to a variety of reasons. They merged, in large part, because they fundamentally believed that by pooling their resources, talents, and treasures, they could make a greater impact in the lives of individuals and families of the south metro Denver area. Having lived through that experience and having watched God work, there are many lessons we have learned the hard way that will hopefully serve to prevent you from having to learn the same lessons.

Pitfall #1: Lack of Prayer

I realize the simplicity of the principle yet recognize the depth of the challenge. The simple truth is that far too many churches are deciding what type of staff to hire, how big of a budget to set, what type of programs to run, and what kind of philosophy to adapt without taking their marching orders from God.

To give the benefit of the doubt, I am sure there are many church leaders who are striving to succeed with good intentions. But good intentions are not always God's intentions. If you are unwilling to seek God in prayer, then how can you ever know *exactly* what God wants? Had Joshua not heard from the Lord, I am not sure that he would have felt comfortable deciding that the best plan was to simply march around the walls in order to defeat Jericho. It just didn't make any sense.

Similarly, I am not sure that Jonah would have ever gone to the wretched Ninevites. The disciples would have never set out to feed the multitudes with such a small stipend of food. Nehemiah would have stayed in the king's palace, never returning to rebuild the walls around Jerusalem. The lame would have not walked, and the blind would have never seen. Yes, these testimonies of the faith would have been much different if they had not listened to the Lord God. Whether through a bush, in the cleft, on the mountain, or in a valley, we must be willing to listen to God. In today's context, many times that comes through prayer.

Further, when you listen to God, regardless of how crazy the plan seems from a human perspective, you can have confidence that God will see you through to a successful completion. Let me say it another way: when what you set out to accomplish is a direct result of God's direction, you can know that the power of God accompanies you. There is power in the name of Jesus!

Not only that, but consider when the touch of Jesus restored sight? Do you remember when the voice of Jesus raised men from the dead? Do you remember when just merely

Practical Tools for Reinventing the Dying Church

touching the cloak of Jesus healed people? Jesus is still in the miracle-making business, but if the church is going to navigate the treacherous territory of this sinful world and accomplish the Great Commission, it is going to come because we have willingly submitted ourselves to the power of God through prayer.

As one who has been a part of multiple revitalization efforts, I can assure you, your revitalization efforts will surely fall short if you are unwilling to daily and diligently practice prayer. Revitalization is way too tough to do it on your own!

Pitfall #2: Failure to practice shared leadership/ministry

The Bible speaks often of the basic principles of leadership. Yet, all too often we have allowed ourselves to become numb to the impact that leadership has in the church. If you desired to gain an insight into leadership by understanding its definition, you would quickly realize that for every book or article written on the topic, there is a definition given. Every quasi-expert to reputable practitioner who writes on the topic has asserted that if you will follow their definition and theories, you will revolutionize your church or business.

All sarcasm aside, this topic is so vitally important to me. However, it is not because I contend to be an expert on the topic. In fact, God has blessed this generation with such great church leaders that I cannot, should not, and will not begin to assert myself as an authority and thus take away from the respect that they deserve. Rather, my passion comes from a fundamental belief that God uses ordinary people like you and me to bring about His extraordinary purposes.

One of the great lessons I have learned over the years as it relates to revitalization leadership is the need to practice what I call shared leadership. Shared leadership is the collaborative effort of all members of a team, working within their areas of giftedness, utilizing their strengths and being aware of their weaknesses, to exert influence within their organization, to achieve the organization's agreed upon goals and objectives. Simply put, involve other people in the journey!

Let's consider Paul's words in his first letter to the church of Corinth. He says, "If the whole body were an eye, where would the hearing be? If the whole were hearing, where would the sense of smell be? But now God has placed the members, each one of them, in the body, just as He desired. If they were all one member, where would the body be? But now there are many members, but one body" (1 Corinthians 12:17-20)

God has bestowed upon His church individual spiritual gifts. These gifts are to be used for the edification of the body. It makes little sense for a foot to function as an ear, or a nose to function as a hand. Likewise, in the church, giftedness should be seen through the lens of ministry calling and therefore should result in a shared ministry/leadership construct.

As such, we learned much like Moses in Exodus 18, when the ministry/leadership load was shared, we gained strength to last longer and the people experienced peace. So, practically, as a leader, I cast vision and led the people to understand what God was doing. At that point, the encouragers got to work encouraging. The administrators got to work administrating. The teachers got to work teaching. As a senior pastor, I did not do everyone else's job. Everyone played their part, we worked together and we shared the ministry/leadership load.

Pitfall #3: Failure to Protect the Unity of the Church

The Bible likens the role and responsibility of a pastor in the church to the role and responsibility of a shepherd. Very literally, to the sheep, a shepherd is their leader, their provider, their guide, and their protector. Sheep will not rest unless basic needs in their life are met. This includes being free from fear, being free from friction or aggravation, being free from hunger, etc. Every day, sheep walk through the "valley of the shadow of death" and the shepherd is responsible to ensure that the sheep are not in want," that they are able to "lie down in green pastures," and are fearful of "no evil" (Psalm 23).

As you consider the process of revitalizing a church, you must stop to consider the needs of the sheep. As the shepherd, are you aware that revitalization will often cause those in the church family to fear the unknown? The reality is that nobody likes change…including you! Change, or the notion of change, has the ability to bring out the worst in anybody. It was the Israelite children who would have rather died in Egypt as slaves under Pharaoh, than face the unknown realities of freedom. Often, church members express the same realities. They would rather live in the securities of what is comfortable, than to venture into the unknown.

As a shepherd, are you aware that revitalization will often cause those in the church family to begin to turn on one another? As decisions are made, people begin to align themselves with one side or another. Lines are drawn, statements are made, feelings are hurt, and friction is abounding. This is how Satan divides a church. As a shepherd, it is your responsibility to ward off the attack of the enemy. Paul says that the body is one unit; it may have many parts, but it is one body (1 Corinthians 12:12). Your physical body works best when each part of the body fulfills its function and works in unity with the rest of the body. So it is in the body of Christ. Shepherds must protect that unity.

As a shepherd, help your sheep process change, deal with change, and carry out change. We should be mindful, unity does not mean complacency. The revitalizer is compelled by God to help the church see and achieve a brighter future, a clearer vision, and a motivating mission. Therefore, a shepherd leader does not give the sheep what the sheep think they need; they give the sheep what the shepherd knows they need. In church revitalization, change is often necessary. However, we don't have to sacrifice unity on the

altar of expediency, pragmatism, or personal preferences.

Pitfall #4: You take Criticism Personally

If you have thin skin, you might want to think twice before leading in a massive revitalization project. Despite your effort in keeping people unified through a revitalization project, there are some who will choose to go the opposite direction. When they make that choice, they will try and rally support and they will convince some to walk the road of dissention with them. At that point, get ready…

At Cornerstone, when we were in the process of merging two churches, there were very few areas of life that proved to be off limits from those who were in disagreement with what was happening. As a result, we got to deal with some of our best friends in the church starting a "stay where we are committee." At the time, I did not think it could get much worse. But, I was wrong! Over a period of months, multiple attacks were leveled on my leadership, people criticized my wife, lawyers were brought in to make threats, a lawsuit was filed, and I got to read an article on the front page of the Denver post, outlining a litany of lies concerning myself and the merger. Yet, in it all, what I learned was that hurt people, hurt people.

Though I was tempted many times to want to take the criticism personally, the reality was that many people were just hurting. They loved their church the way it was. They did not see the need for change. They did not want to give up their program, their philosophy, or their building. Who else or where else could they aim their criticism? By taking criticism personally, I would run the risk of taking my focus off of the task at hand and begin to get into the weeds, where I didn't belong. Bitterness toward the offenders will cause you to fight a battle with those people, not the battle that is really waged against Satan. Listen to criticism, learn what you can, leave the rest, and move forward.

Pitfall #5: Failure to Preach the Word of God

God's Word is a story of revitalization. In fact, when you really stop to think about it, starting in Genesis 3 where we see man's ruin, God begins the process of bringing about his remedy. The redemption of man's heart is revitalization at its greatest. Yet, throughout Scripture we see great stories of revitalization. Consider Abraham, Moses, the prophets, Nehemiah, the ministry of Jesus, the disciples, the ministry of Paul…so many great examples of revitalization.

Practical Tools for Reinventing the Dying Church

This may come as a shock to you, but many within your church don't need to hear what you learned at your last conference or webinar. What people in the church are desperate for today is a word from God. People need to see revitalization through the eyes of God. Ironically, your greatest tool for revitalization is not a survey, poll results, outside experts, or current trends. Your greatest tool is Scripture and so therefore, preach the Word!

A Concluding Thought

I am a fanatical believer in the life of the local Church! I realize that there are some who have given up on the church for multiple reasons. However, not only have I not given up on the Church, I (and likely you) find myself energized at the thought of helping the Church to become all she was intended to be in the eyes of God. Why? For starters, the Church is the only institution in history with a mission and a message which ultimately has the ability to change one's eternal destiny. Therefore, it can be said that the Church has an eternal mission. Think about that for a moment. There are millions of organizations throughout history who are working to make your here and now as good as possible. But, the influence of the local Church has the ability to impact you for an eternity. That is an awesome reality!

From my time in the church, study of the church, and thinking about the church, there is one lesson that I am growing more and more convinced of: *All church growth, church health, church vitality, and church revitalization plans hinge on the simple reality that the people of God must have their hearts captivated by God.*

Show me a church that is captivated by God and you will find a church that has powerful worship, active evangelism, and is on mission, disciple producing, and strong! Show me a church that is captivated by budgets, programs, traditions, buildings, or philosophies and I will show you a church that is confused, bewildered, anemic, plateau, declining, and unhealthy. As leaders in the local Church, we must make it our aim to help people be captivated by God.

Mike Atherton is the Senior Pastor Cornerstone Church in Lone Tree, CO. Dr. Mike has served as a senior pastor for 15 years. Leading a church in a church merger, he has learned firsthand the challenges of a church revitalizer. He has earned a Doctor of Ministry degree with an emphasis in preaching and working on a PHD in Biblical Ministry from Midwestern Baptist Theological Seminary. He is a nationally certified Church Business Administrator through National Association of Church Business Administrators (NACBA) and is the author of *"The Revitalized Church."* Mike leads a Mentored Master of Divinity program at Golden Gate Baptist Theological Seminary and is the President of Colorado Baptist Convention.

CHAPTER EIGHTEEN
Getting to Know Your Congregation
By Tracy W. Jaggers

There are a lot of helpful tools to use when trying to inspect the community around a church, but how many tools help you know the heart of your present flock? Are you ministering to:

- Blue collar worker? White collar worker?
- Educator? Laborer?
- Anglo? Hispanic? Asian? African American? American Indian?
- Boomer? Buster? Millennial?
- Affluent? Economically stable? Financially destitute?

And the list goes on and on! Knowing who is sitting in the chairs or pews of your congregation, as well as outside the walls of the church, is vitally important. Churches normally reach those who are similar to those within the group. So, how can we ascertain the true identity of those in our congregation? Yes, it is harder than merely gazing at the group this next Sunday. People can mislead and even lie to us every Sunday without ever intending to do so.

Congregational Analysis is a valuable tool in finding the "sweet spot" of ministry within your cultural setting. Demographics are a valuable part of this process. They disclose the broad scope of who is in the community, but do not often define the personality of those already in the building. They don't reveal the character of the "fish" you have already caught. This tool will assist you in knowing the mind and heart of your people so you can be more effective for the Kingdom of God.

If you are into laboriously-helpful resources, I recommend Studying Congregations, edited by Nancy T. Ammerman, Jackson W. Carroll, Carl S. Dudley, and William McKinney. This reference work is filled with helpful information, but is like reading an encyclopedia to determine the time of day. It is definitely worthy of inspectional reading, but I found Chapter

Seven: *Methods for Congregational Study* by Scott L. Thumma to be the most valuable for this topic.

There were some thoughts that gave way to creative additions to the research tools we were already practicing in our Church Revitalization process. From this point forward I will offer you the tools that have fit well in our toolbox for the past few years. I pray they will aid you in identifying what type of listeners you are speaking to each Sunday and how to effectively speak their language.

The Lawless Group **Church Health Survey** (http://www.thelawlessgroup.com/) is a written questionnaire requiring 160 responses to a myriad of subjects in an attempt to discern the strengths, weaknesses, attitudes and perceptions the congregant has of the church as a whole. It focuses on the purposes of the church and determines which purpose(s) need the most energy for the future effectiveness of the body. This is the only tool that requires a consultant. Only a certified consultant has permission to purchase and offer this tool. It is worth the cost and the exploration. The congregants get to offer their praise or concerns.

Second, and in no order of importance or significance, are personal congregant and staff interviews. Asking the same question of everyone gives a baseline that leads to clarity and truth. Studying Congregations gives some great hints for interviewing in Chapter Seven as well.

The **personal interviews** begin by explaining the value of the personal interview. These questions give greater clarity and definition to the survey which is raw data and information-oriented. Confidentiality is ensured. Disclosing the process of using numbers rather than names is reassuring to the respondents. Interviews are requested on the day surveys are taken. The pastor helps to gain a broad section of interviewees. Variables include male, female, age, and length of membership. Once an adequate number of interviewees set appointments, the interviews begin.

Practical Tools for Reinventing the Dying Church

The questions are: 1) How long have you been a member of this church family? 2) What brought you to this church? 3) What does this church do well? 4) What do you believe are the greatest challenges for the future of this church? 5) Are there additional challenges you sense are pressing, but are not as important at this time? 6) In your opinion, how are major decisions made in the church? 7) How is the church's past impacting the present state of the church? 8) In a graded format the next three questions are posed (1-10 with 10 being best) How is trust between staff members? How is the trust level between congregants? How would you rate the overall morale of the church?

Finally, if this church were a restaurant, what restaurant would it be and why? If it were a color, what color would it be and why? If you could choose a preaching message or topic you would like hear, what would be the message/topic and why? What question have I not asked that you thought I would/should? What is the answer to that question?

The responses to the interviews are combined with the raw data of the survey in the report presented to the church at the Congregational Workshop.

Next are **observations and evaluations**. These are not for the purpose of being critical or negative. Observations are to help the church make a great first impression and to correct things that may be a distraction or "turn off" to new guests. Observing the *worship service* can be the most arduous and invasive. Pastors and staff rarely like to think of their work as needing adjustment or enhancement, but we all need positive correction or reinforcement. The entire worship event is examined and adjustments are offered from the start time to the final benediction prayer. Sound, lighting, music, announcements, offering, sermon, invitation, etc. are all examined. No stone is left unturned. Nothing here is sacred or untouchable. The first three are segments of our "Windshield Observation."

Facilities – sidewalks, parking lots, bathrooms, wall decorations, room sizes, floor coverings, nursery cleanliness, child safety, etc. are all placed under the microscope to determine if they are helpful or hurtful to the growth of the church. I have seen walls that are in need of a fresh coat of paint and base boards that have a thick layer of dust and lint. God's house is expected to be clean and safe. Let's make an extra effort to lift up the Lord and His meeting place with His Bride so people are turned to Him and not turned off by us!

Parking – it is a statistical fact; once parking lot spaces are filled to about 80%, guests and irregular attendees feel they are intruding and will turn around and exit the lot. We should provide adequate parking and safe parking. Guest parking should be easily seen and handicap spaces should lead safely to the main entrance. Be sure that you provide clear directions to these special parking areas. They should be near the "Welcome Center". Just a note of irritation to me - if you have a designated "Pastor Parking," put it in the back lot. Guests should be given the best spots and remind your congregation of this often!

The traffic flow should be easily maneuvered, especially if you have multiple services. Adequate time between services to exchange cars safely is a must. I have been to some multi-service churches where the lot is as safe as walking across the Indianapolis racetrack on race day. Offer plenty of time for the exchange of cars between services. What you don't see outdoors is inviting frustration and anger to enter the sanctuary. Remember, there is indoor traffic to contend with as well! Crowds are exciting, but they can also become frustrating. How well do you like someone invading your private space at the theater? Point made!

Signage – do your signs reflect your congregation? Are they old and rusty or are they bright and inviting? Can guests navigate your lot and buildings without needing a GPS? Is guest parking clearly designated? Are the buildings marked for unchurched guests? What does "Building B" mean to a new guest? Nothing of course! Try using terminology that everyone will recognize (Worship Center; Youth Center; Children's Building; Preschoolers, etc.). Make sure signs on roads and highways are kept free of weeds, vines, and

Practical Tools for Reinventing the Dying Church

obstructions. If they need new lettering or paint, do not wait until you get a call from Code Enforcement before you do something about the condition of your signage. People often judge a church by its social media presentation and signage. Give paramount effort to putting your best foot (sign) forward!

While we're on the subject of signs – how definitive are your interior signs? Can someone locate the necessary areas of interest (Worship venue; nursery; children's area; RESTROOMS)? Have you ever observed retail stores and how they offer copious signs to major areas of need? And, have you ever scorned the grocery store that has inadequate signage? WHERE ARE THE CRACKERS? Let's learn from what we deem desirable and what we loathe.

Technology – many churches have opted to use Facebook instead of a web page. This is acceptable if you remember the vital information that must be a part of any social media site (service times, address, office email, phone number, etc.). Having a Facebook page that is filled with sweet sayings and Christian videos is nice but doesn't really draw the unchurched to a point of salvation or involvement. Being genuine about who the church is and what type of ministries you offer is imperative. Churches that promise a high-energy, innovative worship experience and don't deliver on Sunday are deceptive. We must never present ourselves or our church as something bigger or better than we regularly deliver. Yelp is a way to advertise similar to an online Yellow Page ad. Of course, every social media system has good aspects as well as the questionable ones. Be careful and monitor your site often. Twitter is a good way to keep people up to date on what is happening at your church. With Twitter, the rule of thumb is "Brief is better." You can tell too much! The key questions to ask a healthy social media are: 1) Does it have a valuable purpose? 2) Does it speak genuinely about who we are and why we are here? 3) Can users gain clear information about our organization? 4) Does it honor the Lord and draw others to Him?

Security Protocol – Having clear, well-described safety plans and processes are critical. Are children checked in and checked out securely? If not, research processes that other churches use and have proven to be safe and successful. Do you have an active-shooter strategy? How are your facility and parking areas secured when services are in progress? Here are a few things to consider: 1) When a crisis occurs who is the voice of authority? 2) Do all workers have to submit to a background check? If not, why! 3) Do you have an emergency action plan? Who calls 9-1-1? 4) Are your greeters and security team members trained in how to de-escalate a suspicious or hostile individual in a non-threatening way? 5) Do you have emergency response personnel and supplies? The worst plan is NO plan.

Secret Shopper Evaluations – inviting three to five couples/families, unknown to the members of the church, to visit a struggling congregation on several consecutive Sundays can give you a strong picture of the church's attitude and normal function. The shoppers must go with the recognition that they will need to detail their experience. Ask them to write down impressions of their visit. Have them fill out a short survey about features they felt revealed quality ministry and what they sensed needed adjustment to be a contender for a return visit. Try to use groups representing multiple generations and some with children and/or youth. This is not to criticize the church concerning their style of worship or ministry, but is about the church's presentation, practices, morale and policies. They will record what they enjoyed and what distracted them or turned them off.

Community Interviews – I love this part! Talking to people in the area surrounding the church divulges oodles about the church's reputation or lack thereof. The interviews are best performed on Sunday as that is the time others will be searching for the church. I train 2-3 church members to go with me to ask the questions (only one gets out of the car with me to ask the questions). Once I had a church

Practical Tools for Reinventing the Dying Church

member in a congregational workshop accuse me of fabricating answers. She almost called me a liar! I do it this way so the members hear directly what the community is saying about their church. The questions are posed to people who would normally be approached by travelers looking for a specific location (gas station attendant; quick stop cashier; fast food worker; grocery store cashier; donut shop sales person; etc.). There are three simple non-threatening questions? 1) "Can you tell me how far I am from <u>name of town/city</u>?" 2) "I am actually looking for a church located in that town. It's called <u>name of church</u>, do you know where it is?" 3) "Have you ever heard of the church, or know anything about it?" Make sure you leave your smartphone in the car or they'll ask why you don't just Google it on your phone. I once had a college-age female employee in a donut shop go get her smart phone and look up the church. She wasn't even aware it was just 2 blocks away – and it was a huge facility! One church member was in tears when she asked about the reputation of her church and found the community thought they were unkind to new guests.

Church Documents/Promo Materials – I worked with a church that had the church meeting times in their Constitution. They couldn't adjust their service time without a two-week, notified meeting and a seventy-five percent affirmative vote. That's crazy! Constitutions are the non-negotiables, the hard-to-change issues (Who the church is; What is the purpose; Statement of beliefs; governance; How to amend; Dissolution). Bylaws are easier to change because they represent function (affiliations; how to join; how to break fellowship; staffing and workers; committees/teams; officers; meetings; format for business; etc.). Make sure the documents free up the church and do not place it in bondage.

Finally, *the congregational workshop* – this is a church-wide, interactive event. Everyone who wants a voice for the future good of the church should show up! The elements of the workshop include:

- "A Healthy Church" presentation

- The survey findings (previously disclosed to the pastor and staff)
- A history of the world – a timeline and discussion
- The history of the church – also on the timeline; recognizing how the world has affected the church
- Discussion of values or purpose - developing a fusion of ideas
- Unpacking the areas of greatest need
- Showing what offers the best hope for the future
- Detecting probable barriers to success
- Gathering possible solutions to the barriers
- Sending the discoveries to the Church Revitalization Team

Gathering these tools, together with a strong demographic package, will aid you in gaining a clear picture of the environmental, sociological and cultural mindset normally found within the walls of your worship center. May these tools help you reach those who have yet to experience your church's Kingdom ministry. We better understand our congregation by listening to their heart. May your entire church family thrive in helping others experience His salvation!

Tracy Jaggers earned his Doctor of Ministry degree in Church Revitalization from Midwestern Baptist Theological Seminary in Kansas City, Missouri. He is a frequent blogger and writer for state and national revitalization websites and magazines, and is an active speaker in state and national revitalization conference.

Chapter Nineteen
Your Best Church Year
How to Have a Breakthrough Year
Ron Smith

Every pastor possesses an enduring crave to see the church accomplish amazing things. These dreams and desires often subconsciously drive their movements throughout their ministry. Yet, these revelations often remain as such. They never transform into recognizable realities because every pastor, at some point in serving, hits the wall of actuality. Actuality is comprised of the challenges that come with guiding a people and a church to realize their unique calling. This actuality is what dampens the strength of that enduring crave, as it becomes buried by discouragement.

What the pastor and the church needs is a breakthrough. Most pastors don'there to start or who to turn to for resources and guidance for this breakthrough. In this chapter I aim to offer such resources. I hope to revive the crave for the calling that exists in all of us serving the church. Over the next few pages we will walk through three stages of breakthrough: physical, psychological and practical. Together we will discuss, review and discover how to have our best church year, taking what is revelation and transforming it into reality.

Breakthrough Conversations: Talking Your Way into the Future
(the physical side)

Let's picture church health like a car – any kind you want, as shiny as you want, as expensive as you want.

When you picture church health like a car, you have to take into account that sometimes it gets stalled. Sometimes it just doesn't seem to go anywhere; no matter what operations you employ to get it going. As much repair cost as you put in, as shiny as it looks on the outside, as expensive as it might be, church relationships sometimes get stalled. The question is, when a church gets stalled, how do you get it going again? Simply, you've got to put the right fuel in.

All relationships are fueled by communication. It's what drives relationships, what makes them run, what makes them work. I don't care how great the relationship looks on the outside. If you're not constantly putting the fuel of communication into the relationship, it's going to get stalled. Look at any relationship that's not working. If you were to pinpoint the exact places where a bridge needs to be built, but has not yet been created, you can guarantee that someone, somehow, someway stopped talking. And whenever that happens, it stalls.

The problem is communication is not an exact science. Remember the class you took in college, Communication Science? It doesn't work that way. I've found that it's not a science. It's actually more of an art. It's not black and white; it's filled with fine lines and shades of color. If it's an art, I feel like a lot of you: a kid with a crayon trying to figure out how to color between the lines. I still have a lot to learn. This is an area where we need an expert to help us learn how to communicate.

Whenever you're in a problem, you need an expert. If your car has a breakdown and you're not a mechanic, hopefully you'll take it to a mechanic, an expert, who will help you fix it. If you have a plumbing problem and you don't know how to fix plumbing, I hope you don't try to do it yourself. You're under the sink, the water's on you and you're thinking, "I should have called an expert!"

There is no one better at the art of communication than Jesus Christ. Ask anybody and they'll say Jesus is a great teacher. He knew how to communicate. Today, I'd like us to look together at what He has to teach us about the art of communication. This is somewhat of a hobby, a fascination, of mine. I spent a number of years studying what He had to say about communication, how to talk to people and what it means for us.

Practical Tools for Reinventing the Dying Church

A close look at the Scriptures reveals that He engaged in many breakthrough conversations. We will briefly mention these and then discuss how to communicate for breakthrough.

First of all, we know that our churches are talking. Your church is talking about church health, growth, finances, change, tradition, worship and so on. Make no mistake about it; your church is talking about something. The goal is to find common conversational ground, to get them talking about the things that will lead the church toward breakthrough. The hope is that as we – a unified body – begin to talk the same talk, consequentially we will begin to walk the same walk, taking healthy, unified steps in the same direction.

Biblical conversations that led to a breakthrough:

Genesis 3:8-13 – The "What Has Happened" Conversation:

Uncomfortable? Yes. Difficult? Yes. Needed? Unquestionably. This conversation needs to happen in our churches. What has happened? Why are we off course? What sin is in the body that is keeping us from moving in sync with the heartbeat of God?

Genesis 12:1 – The "Step Out" Conversation:
Every church, no matter the size or condition, must have this breakthrough conversation before the Lord God. Take a step of faith, and go where you are told to go. The Great Commission for every believer is, "Go!"

Exodus 3 – The "Call" Conversation:
Every pastor had better know they are called into ministry and to that place of service. No paycheck or church size is sufficient enough to cover the call.

Exodus 18 – The "Get Your Act Together" Conversation:
Every pastor has a little bit of Moses in them, attempting to bear greater responsibility over their body than what

they can effectively hold. This conversation for the pastor is a reminder to equip the saints. To the saints, it's a reminder that they have a ministry and that ministry is not just church attendance.

Joshua 24:15 – The "Cross the River" Conversation:
This is probably one of the most relevant revitalization talks. Every church will have that moment when God reminds them from where they have come, where they need to go and issue a call for a choice to be made: choose this day whom you will serve. Will you serve the gods of the past, tradition and programming? Or will you serve the Living God?

Matthew 6:13-20 – The "Who Is Jesus" Conversation:
One of the signs of a declining church is the lack of personal experience with Christ. Most church members can "do" church without Christ. This conversation asks the question, "Who do you say Christ is?" The answer reveals the church's mission and the Christian's heart.

Matthew 28:18-20 – The "What Are We Doing" Conversation:
It's a simple question that can reveal a complicated mess. What are we doing as a church? Is what we are doing fulfilling the Great Commission? If not, why are we doing it?

Despite the potential consequences of having unsuccessful, difficult conversations, there are also significant costs attached to not having the conversation whatsoever.

Not having the conversation has implications for an individual's physiological and psychological health. Failing to have an important conversation can result in an individual experiencing increased
heart rate and loss of sleep, cause undue anxiety

and stress and negatively impact personal productivity.

Practical Tools for Reinventing the Dying Church

In turn, the impact of stress on our bodies can potentially lead to more severe physical conditions, such as depression, diabetes, heart disease and obesity. There are substantial costs on individual health of failing to have difficult conversations.

Successfully mastering breakthrough conversations can have a positive effect on people's careers. Twenty-five years of research has found that individuals who are the most influential – who get things done, while building relationships – are those who have mastered breakthrough conversations.

Research also reveals that church conflicts are directly related to the failure to have and handle conversations about change in a healthy format. Some of the ramifications that arise due to the failure to handle such conversations are:

- Church splits that damage the church's reputation
- High staff turnover
- Loss of morale
- Decreased baptisms
- Increased stress
- Decline in attendance

Guidelines when having breakthrough conversations:

Pray for Timing

As Solomon says, there is a time for everything under the sun. Timing is critical. Pray for timing. Ask the Holy Spirit to reveal the time. Pray for the heart of the person or persons involved. Pray for the environment to reveal itself so you can conduct this conversation more effectively.

Calculate the Outcome

You cannot talk your way into the future if you do not know where you are going.
Don't have a conversation simply to have a conversation. Be prepared to answer the why behind your what. Know why you need to leave Egypt, rebuild the walls, and cross the river. Calculate the outcome of the conversation.

Speak in Truth

Stay scriptural. Keep your conversation scripturally based. Opinions are plenty; convictions are scarce. Scriptural conversation is loaded with the power of God's Word, a force with the ability to enlighten, convict and empower. Use this to your advantage.

Build Trust

This was important to Jesus. Matthew 5:37 says, "Simply let your yes be yes and your no, no. Anything beyond this comes from the evil one." Communication begins by building trust. Without trust, there's no real communication.

Use Your Eyes and Ears (not just your mouth)

Proverbs 18:13 says, "Listen before you answer. If you don't you're being stupid and insulting." Genuine listening is hard work. It's a fully engaged process. The Chinese character for listening incorporates the symbols for eyes, ears and undivided attention all in one character. It's paints a pretty good picture of what listening is all about. It involves all of me.

L – Look at people
I – Invest in people
S – Stop whatever you're doing
T – Think about what they are saying
E – Empathize with them
N – Notice body language

What do you talk about?

Talk about the God of Abraham, Isaac and Jacob. Share the story of God's presence, provision and promises. Talk about the mission of the church. Talk about taking steps of faith, following Christ and reaching people. Talk about the community, who they are, what they struggle with and what they do on Sundays. Talk about choices. We can keep doing laps around the desert, or we can cross over. We can listen to a giant mock our God, or we can slay the giant. Talk about how we can choose to either live in the comfort of traditions and the safety of membership, or we can get the message out.

Ask questions that inspire action. How do we get the message out? What does a living church look like? Would lost people believe in what I follow? Is our church a place where the lost and hurting can come and find life and hope and joy and peace? Have you found life and hope and joy and peace in our church? What if the twelve operated church like we do? Would the gospel have spread around the world?

Having breakthrough conversations lays the groundwork for the actual work of revitalization. As soon as you begin the conversation it is essential to deal with the psychological and emotional aspects of change. Often what makes sense mentally may not make sense emotionally. Many times I have had conversations with church leaders who "talk the talk" but not "walk the walk." In exploratory conversations with them, here is how they stated the dilemma they were experiencing: "Pastor, I get it up here (pointing to their head) but I don't get it here (pointing to their heart)."

Intellectually they understood that change needed to happen, that being Biblical was the right thing. But emotionally they could not get past the feelings of comfort, heritage and tradition. The language was in the head, but change wasn't in the heart. As change agents in the work of ministry, we must deal with the psychological side of breakthrough by building, capturing and riding those moments of change through the duration of our work.

Breakthrough Change: Riding the Wave of Revitalization (the psychological side)

First, look through and beyond your current environment. If you simply stare at the mountains, the sea and the chariots, your situation will seem impossible. Discouragement is the greatest tool of the devil, and he is not afraid to use it. Every one of us, as change agents, is called to "put things in order" (Titus 1:5). But, we can only do so when we acknowledge the environment before us, aim for the transformation of the environment beyond us, and ask for the church to encounter this environment beside us.

Having an understanding of what you are facing is crucial, but being able to see beyond it is critical. As you gain the trust of the church and as they begin to follow you they need to know that crossing the Red Sea is worth it. You are going to need them to see it, support it and cross with you.

Next, develop a potential mindset.

See the potential in people. None of us inherit a church with all the right leaders in the right places ready to serve. Jesus spent three years with twelve men, some of whom we would probably deem unfit to serve in our own churches.

We need to see their potential and they need to see their potential. The reason the children of Israel left Egypt was the hope of a preferred future. Yet, because they neglected to recognize their potential – the potential to experience the greater things that lied ahead – they limited themselves by stopping to slump in hindsight, as they glanced at what was behind. A church is in need of revitalization when they love the comfort and convenience of the place they occupy. But by directing their attention to the potential they possess, comfort no longer becomes the primary emotion. Instead, ease is replaced with empowerment. And the church moves forward.

Beginning the work of revitalization will undoubtedly focus on the things that aren't working and what needs to change. If we are not careful this can be overly negative. Helping the church see the potential for greater works, greater days and an incredible future will help the church remain in the work when the work seems long and doubts arise.

Finally, model the ministry you desire.

Be Expectant for Great Things to Happen

Create an environment of expectation. Say things like: "So excited for Sunday." "Looking forward to next week's message." "We are ready for VBS." "Our kids are preparing something great."

Be Excited

Be happy, smiling, optimistic, humorous and helpful. In this psychological and emotional phase of breakthrough, the contagious emotions of joy and happiness can act as vessels that deliver the communication of breakthrough and the challenge for breakthrough more accessible to the church. If the mind is ready to receive a message of breakthrough, it will be manifested in a ministry of breakthrough.

Be an Encourager

"People like cheerleaders more than bosses." Here are some ways to express encouragement: Watch your church and point out the good. Use your words. Share stories. Bless your people. When you bless your people, you are actually building the future.

Write about it. Send cards, notes and emails.

Be Double-Visioned – Look Beyond and Invest in the Future. This is an add-on to seeing the potential. As a leader, you need to begin leading with double vision. If you are running 100, then begin planning for 200. You must see the growth before it happens and make plans to be ready for growth. You might not double overnight, but if five or ten more people show up, would you be ready for them? Demonstrating that you are prepared for any amount of growth communicates that you are ready for more growth. Prepare for health, growth and life.

Here is quick list of how to lead with double vision.

Communicate the State of Ministry

Constantly share the good news of the church. Remind them of their Commission (Matthew 28:18-20) and remind them of why they are on this journey.

Motivate through Your Messages

We can do this. We must step out. Taking steps of faith is what we do. All of these encouraging statements are needed as you develop a needed sense of revitalization.

Equip the Body for Ministry

Getting people involved and excited is priceless.

Learn How to Develop Stewards

If you write the agenda, you need to know how to underwrite the agenda. Do not shy away from preaching on Biblical stewardship.

Celebrate

People love to celebrate. Have fun in ministry.

Utilize Testimonies

Let others share their good news.

Breakthrough Challenge: 11 Ways to Revitalize the Future of the Church
(the practical side)

There are common denominators in every renovation scenario. I have found these 11 ways are proven and practical elements that will change your church now and for the future.

1. Have the Ability to Say No

Vision needs clarity. Clarity determines what we say yes and no to. Having the ability to know when to say no is an indicator that your vision is clear. Think of it this way: when you go to the ophthalmologist, he presents an image before each eye and repeatedly asks a series of questions. "Yes or no?" "Better or

Practical Tools for Reinventing the Dying Church

worse?" In asking the right questions, you are able to gauge where your vision might not be clear. But, answering the right way is just as important. If you just continued to say yes to the ophthalmologist, you would be misidentifying the areas where your vision is not clear. Answering no might not be easy, but as leaders it's a necessary part of refining and maintaining healthy vision.

2. Get Outside the Box

Houdini was a master at demonstrating the power of going outside the box. He knew that death would come if he stayed in the box. Know how to get out of the box and then do it.

3. Establish a Culture of Decision-making

There are four types of decision-making styles.

1. Command Decisions – when decisions need to be made on the spot
2. Collaborative – team feedback decisions
3. Consensus – body decisions
4. Convenience – when someone else needs to make the decision

All four of these styles need to comprise your decision-making culture. Each style meets a different need and reaches a conclusion in a different way. Use each to fit the needs of your specific situation.

4. Maintain Flexibility

Overcome and adapt. "Blessed are the flexible, for they will not be bent out of shape." Culture moves fast. Life is predictably unpredictable. There needs to be an awareness of the need for flexibility. If we are not careful, we can fossilize in our systems and ways of operation.

5. Make This Day That Day

Of all the advantages a leader holds it is the ability to see where they are going.
Seeing what needs to happen in order to move forward is a great thing; it helps lay the groundwork. Start leading, planning and equipping like you are more than what you are. In doing so, when you get "there" you can handle the increase. Lay the groundwork and the need for: staff, rooms, ministries, events and budgets. Frequently ask "what if" questions: What if we see 20 new families? What if 100 visitors came on a Sunday? What if we start turning families away because of our nursery, children's area and student ministry? Plan today like your tomorrow is here.

6. Become Contagious not Religious

Faith is contagious. Excitement is contagious. Joy is contagious. Smile; be happy; be genuine. Celebrate not complain. Love instead of condemn. Lift up instead of load down. Offer grace instead of grumble, and you will attract people Be a church where people want to invite people to attend.

7. Embrace Social Media

The first automobile instructors had a hard time getting people to press the brake. It's always been difficult learning new advancements in technology, and even harder learning to adapt them to our current cultures. It may be hard to imagine, but social media is here to stay. Find someone who understands it. Post something once a day on Facebook (Scriptures, pictures, quotes from different works you are studying, etc.). Have someone take pictures and post them. Social media is a free public relations campaign in your hands. It's free fellowship. It's fast fellowship, and its effects last much longer than the moment.

8. Value Experimentation

If the horse is dead, dismount. Remind the church that failure is more common than success. Did Noah have any experience building a boat? Did Abraham have any experience navigating to the Promise Land? Did Peter know how to walk on water? We must continually tweak current ministries and try new ones.

9. Move from Membership to Ownership

Arthur Flake was a master of his time. He did more to grow Sunday School ministry than any other man I am aware of. In one of his works, I discovered six points of ownership that Arthur Flake instilled in the hearts of those in his ministry: attending regularly, being on time, bringing their bible, contributing to the offering, preparing a lesson, and attending services. What Pastor would not be pleased if their church members came to church with that attitude? Membership in ministry engages people. Ownership in ministry empowers people.

10. Adjust People's Priorities not Just Their Schedules

The early church did more than add a time of worship and house meetings to the schedule. The early church changed people's priorities about God, life and mission. Teach the value of living life on mission. Schedule times of living life on mission. Get them serving, often, with impact. Show them a preferred future.

11. Practice 52 Quality Sundays

Act as if this Sunday is someone's first. Emphasize quality and quantity. Put your best forward on Sunday. Sunday is indeed the first day of the week, despite cultural norms. Train your church in this philosophy: if we get Sunday right, we get the week right. If we get God right, we get everything else right. Sunday needs to be a win for everybody. Define the win for your leaders, for your members, for your visitors and for your mission. Ask: what will make an impact on the lives of those who attend? Do not ask: what will they like? What will make them happy?

The church has a future as you can see. We can follow these 11 principles right now and see immediate results. After five turnarounds, I have found these three breakthrough aspects to be a vital catalyst in moving the church in the right direction. I, like you, am an everyday pastor of the local church and I have discovered, in every level of growth and change, I am constantly implementing the physical, psychological and practical aspects of effective change, aiming toward health and growth.

We all need those breakthrough moments in our ministries. They keep us going. They keep us alive. They keep us praying, studying, ministering and dreaming of what God might be able to do. I am persistent in believing this will be your best church year yet.

Dr. Ron Smith is the Lead Pastor of WaterStone Church in Longwood, Florida. Ron has served as a pastor for over twenty years, revitalizing churches in the Southeast, Midwest, and West Coast. Ron has developed the small church, the stuck church, and the mega church. Ron is known for passionate, biblical preaching and visionary leadership. Additionally, he serves as Co-Leader of the *Renovate One Day Training* with Tom Cheyney helping churches and leaders in the greater Orlando area. Ron is the author of *Churches Gone Wild*. Recently Dr. Smith has taken over from Tom Cheyney the virtual coaching of church revitalizer's through the Renovate Virtual Coach Network to allow time for Dr. Cheyney to focus on the Renovate Church Revitalization Bootcamps.

CONCLUSION
Elements Most Critical for a Church to Turn Around
By Tom Cheyney

There are elements and ingredients that are essential to the turning around of any church. This list can appear to be endless, since each situation is to some degree unique and unlike even a neighbor's church. What binds these elements all together is the presence of the Holy Spirit and an openness of the people to the working of God's Spirit. Here are some common elements most critical for church renewal:

A Pastoral Love for His People.

The role of the turnaround pastor is to be so committed to the people that they recognize his unconventional determination to be one of them, not simply a rescue expert. For a church to turn around, it must not be allowed to develop a pastor-of-the-week syndrome. The pastor must be able to make an honest and convincing commitment to see the congregation through to the end, whether in success or failure.

Select a New Pastor.

In the vast majority of cases, the former pastor is too associated with and injured by the decline to be able to reverse it. A new pastor is usually necessary to create the climate and the plans for a successful resurrection of the congregation.

Release the Past.

It almost goes without saying that to survive and thrive, a congregation must focus on the future rather than relive the past. But this is easier said than done. It requires a new or renewed vision. This is another reason why a new pastor is often necessary. You must honor the past but not live in the past and new pastors can make an easier transition towards that outcome then those who have been there for a long time.

Define Outreach.

To reverse a decline caused in part by an inward focus of ministry, congregations must intentionally define what outreach the church will emphasize.

Equip the Congregation.

Intentional outreach will fail to renew a congregation if done only by the only the pastor and staff. Therefore, the laity must be trained for effective, targeted ministry. If the laity will not embrace their part of outreach the church is in danger of closure even before the revitalization efforts get launched.

Select a Strong Leader.

Declining congregations that hired chaplains, caretakers, healers, managers, administrators, or consensus builders fail to gain ground. The most critical skill of the revitalization leader is to help the congregation establish a new vision to which all can commit.

Hard Work.

The pastor and everyone else in the congregation must commit to working hard. This is not to say that Spirit has no role, but that much effort is required to overcome the downward inertia.

There Must Be a Prayer Covering.

If people don't commit themselves to prayer, they will not catch the vision.

You Must Preach Quality Sermons, Not Bible Studies.

Sermons need not be excellent, but they need to be more relevant and inspired than what they are likely to have been during the latter part of the church's decline.

Practical Tools for Reinventing the Dying Church

Seek an Outside Perspective.

Access to objective, outside opinion is critical.

A Committed Core Group.

In addition to a pastor willing to stay no matter what, there must be a core group of lay people with the same commitment.

These are elements and ingredients that are essential to the turning around of any church. While you might be able to eliminate one or two of them, usually the ones most often sought to be eliminated are those that take the most work out of the laity. When those are eliminated there is little chance for a church to grow when the laity abandons the work of the ministry.

APPENDIX ONE
Key Church Revitalization and Renewal Definitions
By Dr. Tom Cheyney

While the field of church revitalization and renewal is ever expanding, along with key definitions relating to this field, here are some of the key fundamental definitions relating to the field of study:

Absence of the Serendipitous Moment: The more a church is under stress the less it feels God's presence! Do not hear me say that God abandons stuck churches, rather I believe the whirlwind, earthquake and conflagration of a church in turmoil makes it all the more difficult to perceive the still small voice of a holy God. The greater the anxiety, conflict, and unyielding stagnation in a congregation, the less the church experiences those serendipitous, coincidental little miracles which seem to indicate the presence of the Holy Spirit alive and at work with one's church.

Adoption: When a stronger healthy church is willing to embrace a sick and declining church to help it get back on its feet and growing again. Usually a covenant takes place between the adopting church and the church being adopted through a covenant.

Affinity Churches: When churches use marketing preferences interests as an instrument to reach a specific target demographic these are referred to as affinity churches.

Agravilles: These are the rural farm service towns where agriculture, forestry, or mining is the predominant industry.

Annual Church Profile: The Annual Church Profile or ACP is a report that a local congregation completes each year and sends to its local Baptist association. In turn the local association passes the information along to the state convention, and eventually to the national convention. The Annual Church Profile (ACP) process exhibits the voluntary cooperation between local churches, associations, state conventions and the national entities.

Practical Tools for Reinventing the Dying Church

Anxiety Shock Absorber: The leader who wants to bring about revitalization change in a congregation must become an anxiety shock absorber. A person with this quality can successfully resist the avalanche of anxiety which is bowling over everyone else within the fellowship. If you stay calm and demonstrate that you are not going to let the process of revitalization and renewal get derailed, it usually has a calming, quieting effect on the entire church.

Assimilation: Personal renewal precedes and leads to corporate revitalization. It's about changed people who courageously change structures. For deep change to come to an organization, its leaders must first go through a process of deep, personal change.

Bella Karoly Principle: In response to church revitalization changes, everybody loves you when you are mediocre but real change agents will be criticized for their hard work and commitment to renewal.

Biotic Capacity: The highest number of people a church can intuitively reach given its available assets.

Bi-Vocational Minister: When a minister does not serve the church on a full-time basis and has a full-time secular occupation.

Blocker: The Blocker is one who struggles with changes and methodologies. They will often work towards defeating something mainly because of possessing the ability to handle change.

Breakthrough: Positive change occurs when we uncover the work of God and align ourselves to His purposes. Most people learn best through discovery. The ultimate discovery of God's vision is the key to facilitating deep and lasting change in the local congregation.

Catalytic Event: As a church deals with its stuckness, most often it will see in the reoccurring patterns that the church will be lead back to a catalytic event which serves as a critical moment from which the germs of paralysis begin to take hold of the church fellowship. The principle is that the negative patterns in a church's life began at an event or a small series of events, which radically and perpetually altered the life of the congregation.

Change Agent: Is one who seeks to make changes in accordance with a pre-developed strategic plan in an effort to revitalize and renew a dying church. These individuals work towards engaging others in a new norm of growth and advancement while managing people's resistance and anxieties.

Church Cul-de-sacs: A church cul-de-sac is when you turn to the left or the right and find your church is in a continual circle moving but with no real advancement. These are the churches which are prime for restarts.

Church Cut-Off: A church cut-off is a relationship which has been indefinitely, perhaps even permanently severed.

Church Deserters: These individuals are basically made up of three types of church attenders, which bring harm to any church revitalization effort. They are those, which merely sit back and look over the church passing judgment on what is or is not happening. The first one is the lay looker, which are there for a time but are gone just about the time you get to know their name. Then they are followed by the Lay Leavers which are gone at the first hint that more is going to be expected from them then had been expected in the past. The last group of church deserters is the Lay Losers. Lay Losers are the ones which want everything to be a win-lose for their point of view and opt out of the renewal effort as soon as their side cannot win.

Church Genograms: are those diagrams of family trees that filter in and out of the congregation. These include those who are longtime members, active members, weekly attenders, and those who have a mere casual acquaintance with the church during special events.

Practical Tools for Reinventing the Dying Church

Church Growth Movement: This term means different things to different people who use it. As used in this series, it refers to the movement, which began in the 1960's primarily through the inspiration of Dr. Donald A. McGavran. It refers to a comprehensive way of understanding the growth and spread of the Christian movement. This movement brought missionary practices to the western hemisphere. Its fundamental tenet was that God intended the church to grow.

Church Revitalization Assistance Team: This team works to help the struggling church in decline to begin to develop tools necessary for the turnaround of a dying or plateaued church. It is usually made up of outside individuals from the church being assisted as it takes much energy and synergy that declining churches usually have not maintained.

Church Revitalization Cluster Groups: Cluster groups offer pastors from multiple churches who are involved in the Church Revitalization Coaching Network to become part of this continuous learning cluster that includes other active church revitalizing pastors going through the network coaching to collaborate together. The renewal pastor can continue being a part of this cluster as long as the church continues to work on its recommendations or up to 36 months.

Church Revitalization Coaching Network: provides a skilled renewal coach who works directly with individual pastors and churches who desire assistance as well as willing to go through a Church Renewal Journey and accept the recommendations provided by the Church Revitalization Network. This coach will provide a listening ear, ask pertinent questions, and expect accountability in fulfilling the recommendations. This process is a three-year journey and churches can become involved once a year beginning in May. The strength of this network for churches in need of revitalization is the weekly interaction with key practioners, monthly coach to the church peer learning group, and a practioner coach available daily if needed for guidance.

Church Revitalization Definition: Church Revitalization is a movement within in protestant evangelicalism which emphasizes the missional work of turning a plateau or declining church around and moving it back towards growth.

Church Revitalization Initiative: Is when a local church begins to work on the renewal of the church with a concerted effort to see the ministry revitalized and the church become healthy.

Collaborative Leader: Is the leader who allows those he works with to assist in making decisions based on their involvement in the decision-making process.

Concentric Circles: Circles within circles are called concentric circles.

Conflict: is a problem to be solved that includes personalities and emotions which have lined up in opposition to each other. In fact, a conflicted situation usually contains multiple problems.

Conflict Avoidance: is the refusal to acknowledge and/or deal with conflict.

Conflict Crisis: is the eruption and outburst that happens in a crisis due to unresolved agendas.

Conflict Hibernation: is hidden below the surface, and is generally peaceful, but problems will resurface later with greater intensity if they are left unresolved.

Continuous Learning Community: are small groups of individuals who come together in a learning environment for an extended period of time led by trained facilitators. They focus on leadership teaching, accountability and peer mentoring.

Controlling Leadership: Is when the church leadership quits providing spiritual direction and begins to operate as organizational controllers.

Consumer Christians: Church hoppers which move from church to church to church seeking the latest feel good easy worship moment over the hard task of renewal.

Practical Tools for Reinventing the Dying Church

Cosmology: Another word for worldview. It describes how people look at and seek to interpret the world around them.

Creative Programming: Constant creativity, the willingness of a church to dare something new in worship or to risk being led by a different person or different sort of person is an indication of real life in a congregation.

Custodians: are church leaders, which have become masters of inactivity within the local church. They fear changes, fail to adapt to changing environments, and eventually lead the church into death.

De-Churched: The expression given to people who have had damaging incidents within a local church and are no longer active in church in general.

Declining Church: Is any church that at one point in time flourished, but now faces spiritual, physical, and numerical failure and is in danger of being dissolved.

Demographics: Demographics are simply characteristics about a population of people. They are used in market research and by governments. Commonly examined demographics include gender, race, age, disabilities, mobility, home ownership, employment status, and even location. Demographic trends describe the historical changes in demographics in a population over time (for example, the average age of a population may increase or decrease over time). Both distributions and trends of values within a demographic variable are of interest. Demographics are about the population of a region and the culture of the people there.

Dictatorial Leader: A leader which functions as a commander and operates from a Tyrannical position.

Dropout rate: New and longtime church members are leaving for other churches in the community, or they are leaving the local church completely.

E-0 Evangelism: Used to describe outreach among nominal church members. There is no increase in church membership when they come to Christ because their names are already on church rolls.

E-1 Evangelism: Used to describe outreach among non-believers who are in the same cultural group as those doing the evangelizing.

E-2 Evangelism: Used to describe outreach among non-believers who are culturally "near neighbors". They may speak a related language though it might not be mutually understood. An example would be German, French, English and Spanish people who have a similar cultural background even though they may not be able to understand one another's language.

E-3 Evangelism: Used to describe outreach among non-believers who are very different from our own cultural group. Their language, customs and worldview are completely foreign to us. These are our culturally distant neighbors.

Emperor's New Clothes Phenomenon: The inability to see in our subconscious the obvious realities all around us.

Entrance Points: are those unique opportunities for connection a local church has which will draw prospects into the church. Most stuck churches need to add a minimum of eight new entrance points into the church to begin a movement towards turnaround.

Ethnicity: The characteristics of a given ethnic or people group.

Evangelization: For our purposes within church revitalization, evangelization takes place when the Gospel has been presented in such a way that those hearing it are capable of making an intelligent decision - yes or no - regarding Jesus as Lord and Savior.

Fairviews: These are the rural towns supported by the blessing of recreational amenities such as: Skiing, fishing, water sports, beaches, lakes, and retirement communities. Some are

Practical Tools for Reinventing the Dying Church

institutional towns where a college, prison, or military base is located and is the primary supporter of the economy.

Fault Lines of Renewal: Renewal fault lines are the merging points, the weakest links, which give way in a local church when the underlying forces become too much to handle. As opposing sides cease to coexist with one another, they will begin tearing the church apart. The distracting symptoms which are not the real issue, are really only the fault lines in the church renewal struggle. They are not the underlying problems, but symptoms which emerged in the midst of revitalization.

Fringe Participants: As a failing marriage between the church and the pastor begins, often a leader in trouble will begin to place huge emphasis on the fringe participants in hope to revitalize his leadership status within a church. Remember we do not call them fringe participants for nothing. Fringe participants are less active, committed, and supportive of the real needs of the church.

Gatekeepers: some hold church power by keeping things from happening, preventing or allowing issues to be aired or addressed. Tenure is often a way a gatekeeper exercises control.

GOAL Pastoral Leadership Development: The Greater Orlando Adventures in Leadership Pastoral Leadership Development is a voluntary, two year, small group, peer learning experience for pastors that involves trained coaching, in-depth reading and mutual encouragement. It provides pastors with various tools for training laity and helps them develop strategies and skill sets for congregational transformation. It further develops the leadership competencies of pastors to enable them to better lead themselves, and their church.

Ground Zero: In order to get to where you want to go you must know first where you have come from. You need to discover the churches ground zero! Once you have discovered where the churches past have been you will be better able to move it forward into a better future. It is imperative that you take a realistic look at where your church stands in relation to health, present challenges as well as opportunities! Understanding your "Ground Zero" is the beginning of the journey and not the end.

Habit Handicap: We do what we are used to doing. We do what usually works. Whatever pattern we fall into, we go there because that is where we are on familiar ground. Ingrained habit combined with the stress response of our system put us at the mercy of our own dysfunctional default settings. We are stuck in a pattern of ineffective behavior.

Health: Healthy churches produce more and better disciples. Church health is about creating an ongoing culture of renewal and life. A healthy church will be a growing church naturally.

Historical Drift: The term utilized to describe the predisposition for organizations to depart over time from their foundational beliefs and practices.

Historical Knowledge: Stuck churches have a history of how they got stuck and often only those who have historical knowledge will be able to communicate to a church revitalizer possible ways the church became polarized and stuck.

Homogeneous Unit: Used to define a group of people having a collective set of characteristics. They may speak the same language, participate in the same profession or have a similar cultural background.

Incremental Change: is change which is small in scope resulting in only small improvements that are often hard to see and understand their necessity.

Influencer: is anyone who is able to exercise significant influence over the people, the focus or the future of a church, ministry, or organization. Influencers can alter congregational conduct by supporting or boycotting ministries, withholding resources, or using their influence to influence votes.

Intentional Catalyst: Some leaders enter the revitalization process out of need to revitalize a church that had in former

Practical Tools for Reinventing the Dying Church

days been quite effective but through various circumstances has become anemic due to cultural shifts and community transition in the primary ministry area. These leaders usually must work to stabilize the effort and then begin a slow process of bringing health to the work and ministry.

Inwardly Focused: The inwardly focused church has few outwardly focused ministries. Budget dollars in the church are spent on the desires and comforts of its church members. The staff spends most of its time taking care of members, doing maintenance ministry, with little time to reach out and minister to the community the church is supposed to serve.

Leader Dependent: When a church is dependent upon one single leader due to failure to train and equip the laity for ministry the church becomes leader dependent instead of people centered.

Leadership: Everything rises and falls on leadership. Leaders must step forward and catalyze people to a greater passion for God and His purposes. The church can only be changed if its leadership is strengthened and functions effectively through empowerment.

Macro-Community: is the self-governing small township with a populace of 25,000 or less that is capable of delivering its residents with all of their essential needs and services.

Macro-Revitalization: An attempt at church revitalization, characterized by supplying programmatic information to the church and its leadership or offering training, but those which are not immediately or directly involved with them.

Mega-Community: is an urban center with a populace of more than 25,000 where large numbers of individuals congregate within its boarders.

Mega-Church: is the church that is located within a mega-community with a massive population at its fingertips. It is a body of believers with many thousands within a few mile grid.

Micro-Church: is the local church, which is located within the macro-community, that is able to deliver to its congregants all of their spiritual and related needs from one singular church body.

Micro-Revitalization: An attempt at church revitalization that is personally involved with the local church and its key leadership in an ongoing affiliation of sponsorship, partnership, supervision, mentoring, and coaching.

Maintainer: The maintainer desires the enhancement of the current state.

Manipulative Leader: A leader functions as a controlling force and seeks to hard sell his followers into what he desires. Ministry by coercion is the fashion of this type of leader.

Manipulators: are church leaders which are quite active in the local church as they place their own personal needs above the needs of the congregation. Members under this form of leadership become merely tools in a game played by those who seek personal reward.

Matriarchs: Like the patriarchs in a church, these are long term leaders that have been in a local church and have gained a degree of leadership priority through tenure. These individuals are not as strong as the patriarchs but have been given similar influence by the patriarchs due to similar beliefs and willingness to align with the former group.

Mergers: Is when a healthy church seeks to merge another unhealthy church into full membership. This is where the two shall become one. Rarely does it actually happen this way. Mergers are friendly take overs for the best of the Kingdom and both parties. Remember that 50 plus 50 does not equal 100! It usually equals 65.

Mighthavebeenvilles: These are the small town hamlets just outside of the agravilles. These are often pastored by ministers just out of seminaries as a first place to serve and develop experience. Usually they are supported by another line of work and bivocational.

Practical Tools for Reinventing the Dying Church

Missional Church: is designed to connect with the different cultures around them and reach out into their target community. They take the church out of the red brick building and into the community. The opposite type of church is the Receptor Church which is designed to hold those who find the church rather than those who the church discovers.

Momentum Takers: This is the type of leader who is more in it for themselves than they are in it for those they serve.

Never-Churched: The term attached to individuals who have never been involved in the life of the church.

Normative Church: Is the church within the western hemisphere which is the normal size congregation found in the populace. In North America that normal size is somewhere around 150 weekly church attenders.

Nostalgia Churches: These are dying churches living in the past where the emphasis is on tradition rather than advancement. A hopeful return backwards to the church's glory days is what is desired yet once they get there they find it is unrewarding and all-consuming. Nostalgia churches are often more focused on the past and living in past glories then they are present realities. While it is important to honor the past in order to move successfully into the future it is just as important not to live in it! Nostalgia can lead to destruction.

Nudge List: Churches that are falling back into becoming legacy churches often need the nudge to get going again. Think about ideas and ways (nudges) that will send a simple message to the community that you are doing a new thing and doing something new.

Old Blood Congregations: Churches that are older adult-heavy are often prone to ministry failure. Old blood churches tend to focus everything inward, committing all their resources to internal service or maintenance, and slowly become anonymous in their community.

Opinion setters: those who hold the power because of visible influence in decision making.

Outreach/Maintenance Compendium: is when equilibrium between reaching the loss of one's community through outreach and the building up of those who are already saved and part of the local church (maintenance), the congregation will decline.

Paradigm Shift: Pronounced "Para-dime". A paradigm is a framework into which we fit ideas which we hold to be valid. It provides order for arranging how we look at the world. When one changes the primary way he or she looks at the world, we call that "paradigm shift". The most profound paradigm shift for the Christian is the conversion experience.

Pastor Chaplain: The rank and file church member views the pastor as their personal chaplain, expecting him to be on call twenty-four hours a day for their needs and preferences. When he fails to meet their expectations criticism usually follows.

Patriarchs: are long-term church members that lead the church through influence that has been gained from tenure. These are often the most resistant to any change within a local church.

Plateaued Church: is a church that is neither growing nor declining but is in a perpetual state of polarization and unable to move forward to seek health. Such churches have a rate of growth roughly equivalent to the rate of attrition.

Polarization: Creates an organizational climate in which members mistake one another for the enemy and fall into conflict.

Polarized Congregations: Polarity literally means to draw individuals to one pole or another. Therefore, a polarized congregation is one in which it is the tendency of church folks to choose sides. In a polarized church, there are extreme cliques to the point that certain groups of people invariably tend to side together on every issue, tend to distrust other groups, and tend to view themselves as the only steadfast keepers of the flame of truth! Polarized congregations are church splits looking for a reason to happen!

Producers: a successful leader of church revitalization in a local church is called a producer. It is their desire to make things better within the local church. They produce lasting results that enable the church to make the turn towards growth and health.

Rebirth: in the midst of decline and despair when the beginning signs of hope and promise surface, a rebirthing is about to take place.

Receptor Churches: Are churches designed to hold those who find the church rather than those who the church discovers? The opposite type of church is the Missional Church, which is designed to connect with the different cultures around them and reach out into their target community.

Reconciliation: The Bible says that Christ reconciled us to God (Romans 5:10; 2 Corinthians 5:18; Colossians 1:20-21). The fact that we needed reconciliation means that our relationship with God was broken. Since God is holy, we were the ones to blame. Our sin alienated us from Him. Romans 5:10 says that we were enemies of God: "For if, when we were God's enemies, we were reconciled to him through the death of his Son, how much more, having been reconciled, shall we be saved through his life!"

Refocusing: Refocusing is the third pillar and it helps churches that are growing but still need to set new challenges and look for new opportunities to expand their gospel witness into their target area. Questions such as: "What is your Biblical purpose? and "Why do you exist as a congregation?" must be addressed. Looking at how God showed up in the past is a good way to get the church unstuck by addressing where it has been, how God has worked and anticipating what He has for our future. Addressing the church's focus, vision and leading them to discover God's new direction is just the beginning of helping a congregation to begin refocusing towards the Lord's new calling plan for the church! Many a pastor today has never been taught how to grow a church and they feel quite stuck and in need of someone to come along side of them and challenge them to refocus themselves and the church!

Regeneration Pastor: is one who has the revitalization skill sets necessary for assisting a church in its turnaround efforts.

Reinvention: This sixth pillar of Church Revitalization deals with tools and techniques necessary to assist the church when it is necessary to reinvent itself to a changing community. When a church experiences a shift in the community makeup, often there will be to various degrees, the need to redevelop a new experience for those who make up the new context! New experiences must replace old experiences. New practices likewise will replace old practices. A church that is experiencing the need for reinvention must take seriously the need and make the commitment for reinventing itself, revaluing itself, reforming itself, and reinvigorating itself to fit the new context.

Reinventors: The Reinventors are those completely committed to the unceasing radical change necessary to bring about growth and renewal.

Renewal Prayer Team: is for churches that chose to do be part of the Church Revitalization Coaching Network, this internal team will pray regularly for changes that help their congregation fulfill its vision for revitalization.

Renewing: Church Renewal is the fourth pillar of the seven pillars of Church Revitalization process. Often the church simply needs to get back to that which was working and get back on track. When that is needed, a careful renewal strategy needs to be planned and carried out. Renewing a congregation becomes much harder than the refocusing, re-visioning and revitalization process. Not everyone who works in church renewal is wired the exact same way and it is important to understand each congregations' needs and not try to make a one size fit all! Far too much writing on church growth of the 1980's was designed in a one size fits all "Bigger is Better" model and while it may not have been the only cause for declining numbers in our churches, it certainly contributed! It is vital that you prepare the laity for the work of church renewal as well as yourself.

Practical Tools for Reinventing the Dying Church

Communicate early and often with the church how the renewal process will take place and how it will be implemented. Prepare yourself spiritually, prepare your leaders spiritually, then begin preparing your church spiritually for renewal! A Church Renewal Weekend is a great way to start! Church renewal is not about finding the magic medication or treatment to get growing. It is more about discovering God's vision for the church and practicing it for the long haul.

Repetitive Programming: is when a church is chained to the proverbial tether ball going around and around the same old ways without ever seeking new vitality. Once you have gone around and around in a circle long enough you just cannot move forward any longer.

Repotting: This is a kinder friendlier term often used by those in the midst of restarting. It is the same strategy as restarting but some ministers feel they can handle this term better.

Reproduction: A revitalized church is one that is healthy enough to birth new life. Training leaders... parenting churches... helping other churches revitalize. This comes when we understand our place in God's big picture.

RENOVATE National Church Revitalization Conference: A national cross denomination Church Revitalization Conference, which meets annually in November to raise the thought and influence regarding various aspects of church revitalization and renewal. This group and its influencers are working towards creating a Church Revitalization Movement that will raise the level of revitalized churches within the western hemisphere.

Restarting: The final Pillar of Church Revitalization is the hardest and often only happens once the churches patriarchs and matriarchs have tried everything else they could think of to grow the church with no success! When a sick church no longer has the courage to work through the various issues that led to its poor health, it is usually identified as being on life support and in need of a restart. This type of church has been flat lined and just holding on by means of its legacy and the faithful few who attend. Being aware of their "critical" condition, however, is not enough. They have got to become convinced they need "major" surgical treatment. Changing the mindset of the residual membership can be very difficult. Most of these churches are peopled by senior adults. Change is often hard to come by. Until the church is ready to make drastic change, it is useless to become involved. There are thousands of churches like this all over America: Some are Baptists, others are Methodists, even in the Assembly's you can find them, Presbyterians, the Lutherans have them, Congregational, Christian, and many others, waiting for a mission-minded congregation to get involved in offering "new life." It is a startling phenomenon today that there are some laity that, as they begin to depart this life, see nothing wrong with taking the church to the grave as well. That was never part of God's plan for the thing for which He gave up His life.

Restoration: This fifth area of Church Revitalization addresses the issues a church and minister must go through when circumstances necessitate a restoration process. Things such as: gaining a new and fresh understanding of the new prospect for the church which is vital if success is going to be in the church's future; inspiring new prospects with a vision that is both compelling and motivational; meeting new needs in order to give you a restored place among the community where you seek to further minister; become prospect driven during these days of transition looking for new and unreached opportunities to minister; crafting something that comes out of a community in flux and looking for ways to reconnect to the community where you once were firmly entrenched.

Restructuring: The term used to describe the changing of the church structure so that it becomes compatible with the culture in which it is located.

Re-visioning: Have you ever seen a church that once was alive and vital begin to lose its focus and drive for the cause of Christ? That is a church that needs to work on its Re-visioning strategy! Any Re-visioning strategy works to help churches dream new dreams and accomplish new goals that lead towards regrowing a healthy church! This strategy is designed for a weekend retreat tailored fit to foster a sense of ownership and team ship related to discovering a shared vision for the church. Understanding the critical milestones necessary for a new vision will help foster healthy church practices that might have been lost do something as simple of achieving a great goal and God's children taking an ill-advised rest that resulted in a slowing of the momentum into a maintenance mentality.

Revitalization: A church in need of Revitalization is described as one where: there is the plateauing or declining after a phase of initial expansion; the Church experiences the beginning of a high turn-over of lay leaders; there becomes a shorter duration of stay of the fully assimilated people in the work; the church morale and momentum level drops; the church coasts for a brief time and then drops again, only to see the cycle of decline repeated again and again.

Revitalization Players: Those who are willing to count the cost towards church revitalization and seek to add to the churches efforts of renewal. These individuals are mission conscious, servant minded, able to deliver the goods, seek to help others succeed, able to make the tough calls or hard choices, and finish the course well.

Revitalization Pretenders: With the rise of the need for church revitalization in our churches today there are those who would rather act the part and look the part but fall short of fulfilling the part to put in the effort needed for revitalization. These individuals are Revitalization Pretenders who masquerade as being concerned for renewal but are not willing to put in the time or pay the price for revitalizing the church.

Ribbonville: These counties surround a city and often referred to as collar counties.

Sending Culture: creating a sending philosophy is indispensable to revitalizing a church. Churches that are revitalized see themselves as communities on mission with God, not as country clubs for Christians.

Servant Leader: Is a leader which leads through service to others. These leaders exemplify Christ-likeness.

Silver Tsunami: This term refers to the impact of the Baby Boomer generation is making in retirement. These active seniors bring vitality and active lifestyles into churches that have the ability to cater to their needs. A passive style of retirement found in previous generations is not part of this generation.

Skunking: Skunking happens frequently within local church renewal efforts, when pessimistic church members spray negativity all over those creative church members who are trying to spark the renewal efforts of the church. A well-known example would be the tried but true expression by skunkers "We tried that years ago and it did not work."

Sovereignty: A new work of God requires our personal surrender as well as our structures. We must release control and embrace ambiguity. Revitalization is not a "Cookie-cutter" or "program" approach. God's vision for every church is unique and special. Revitalization will look different in each setting.

Steeple Jacking: Occurs when once sizable churches face the pain of shrinking congregants and become vulnerable to congregations with younger participants who become members of the vulnerable church in an effort to overtake their properties. The ambitious healthy church attempts to acquire at little or no cost the buildings and property of the shrinking church. This term refers to when a merger is not a joint effort but more of a hostile takeover.

Strategic change: are changes that usually occur on a large scale within a church body, such as organizational restructuring or governance reconstruction.

Stuck Church: Is a hurting church which displays symptoms of becoming or being stagnant, often paralyzed, numerically declining, strategically dormant, living locked in the past, or dying; it is the opposite of a flourishing and vibrant growing church.

Practical Tools for Reinventing the Dying Church

Synergy: Positive change happens best in the context of relationship. By working together in cohorts for learning and encouragement, progress in the revitalization journey is accelerated, which is mutually beneficial to everyone involved.

Transformational Change: are changes which move the church forward towards a radical, and sometimes unknown, future state of being. It seeks forward movement and leaves past obstacles behind as a new day is in focus.

Three-self Standard: Used to describe indigenous churches which stand on their own two feet. Such churches are often described as being self-supporting, self-governing and self-propagating.

Triangling: is the act of bringing in or drawing in a third party to add stability to a relationship. Adding a third party will often stabilize a relationship, especially if it is an intense relationship.

Unfriendly Take Over: A new type of church merger is arising in the western hemisphere. It is as relatively healthy churches are desperate for partners to validate and credibly reach other cultures, or alliances that can provide resources to expand mission which are unobtainable from denominational or cross-sector sources. These churches usually will force a cultural church to align through some sort of hostile takeover. While there are many healthy churches which are part of friendly takeovers where there is a win- win, it is this last group that ought to be avoided at all costs. A new term defines these hostile takeovers as steeple jacking.

Unfreezing Step: This step requires that individual church members be convinced to give up their old behaviors (forces for change must overcome forces against change) in favor of a new set of church behaviors.

Yesterday's Commentators: One of the biggest challenges to change towards revitalization is the number of Yesterday's Commentators a church possesses. These are the tribe that simply just kills any momentum gained toward renewal through a backwards view that seeks to anchor them in the past unable to make any steps toward the future.

APPENDIX TWO
Suggested Church Revitalization and Renewal Bibliography
The Renovate Group
By Tom Cheyney

Anderson, Hugh. *The Gospel of Mark, New Century Bible Commentary*. Grand Rapids: Wm. B. Eerdmans Publishing Company, 1976.

Anderson, Leith. *A Church for the 21st Century: Bringing Change to Your Church to Meet the Challenges of a Changing Society*. Minneapolis: Bethany House Publishers, 1992.

Anderson, Leith. *Dying for Change: An Arresting Look at the New Realities Confronting Churches and Para-Church Ministries*. Minneapolis: Bethany House Publishers, 1998.

Anyabwile, Thabiti M. *The Life of God in the Soul of the Church: The Root and Fruit of Spiritual Fellowship*. Glasgow, Scotland: Christian Focus Publications, 2012.

Anyabwile, Thabiti. *What Is A Healthy Church Member?* Wheaton, IL: Crossway Books, 2008.

Arn, Charles. *Side Door: How to Open Your Church to Reach More People*. Indianapolis, IN: Wesleyan Publishing House, 2013.

Arn, Win. *The Church Growth Ratio Book: How to Have a Revitalized, Healthy Growing, Loving Church.* Pasadena, CA: Church Growth, Inc., 1987.

Avery, William O. *Revitalizing Congregations: Refocusing and Healing through Transitions.* Herndon, VA: Alban Institute, 2002.

Baker, R. D., Truman Brown, Jr., and Robert D. Dale. *Reviving the Plateaued Church.* Nashville: Convention Press, 1991.

Barna, George. *Grow Your Church from the Outside.* Ventura, CA: Regal Books, 2002.

Barna, George. *Turn-Around Churches: How to Overcome Barriers to Growth and Bring New Life to an Established Church.* Ventura, CA: Regal Books. 1993.

Barrett, C.K. *Acts 1-14, International Critical Commentary.* Edinburgh: T. and T. Clark, 2004.

Basham, Chris and Ken Whitten, North American Mission Board Podcast: Church Revitalization. http://www.namb.net/podcast-church-revtalization/(accessed September 29, 2014).

Batson, Howard K. *Common-sense Church Growth.* Macon: Smyth & Helwys, 1999.

Beasley-Murray, George R. *Word Biblical Commentary, Vol. 36, John.* Waco, TX: Word Books, 1987.

Becker, Paul. *Seeing Your Vision Come True.* Oceanside, CA: Dynamic Church Planting International, 2007.

Benedict, Melanie. "From Embers to a Flame: Revitalizing Churches" *by Faith: The Web Magazine of the Presbyterian Church in America* http://byfaithonline.com/page/in-the- church/from-embers-to-a-flame-revitalizing- churches (accessed October 10, 2010).

Berkley, James D. "Burning Out, Rusting Out, or Holding Out?" *Leadership a Practical Journal for Church Leaders* Volume IV (Winter 1983): 36-40.

Bickers, Dennis. "Bivocational Ministry: Meeting the Leadership Needs of the Smaller Church" *Rev: Revving Up Ministry Together*, November/December, 2008.

Bierly, Steve R. *Help for the Small Church Pastor: Unlocking the Potential of Your Congregation.* Grand Rapids: Zondervan, 1995.

Bierly, Steve R. *How to Thrive as a Small-Church Pastor: A Guide to Spiritual and Emotional Well-Being.* Grand Rapids: Zondervan, 1998.

Blackaby, Henry. *Holiness: God's Plan for Fullness of Life*. Nashville: Thomas Nelson Publishers, 2003.

Blackaby, Henry T., Henry Brandt, and Kerry L. Skinner. *The Power of the Call*. Nashville: Broadman & Holman Publishers, 1997.

Blanchard, Bill. *Church Structure That Works: Turning Dysfunction Into Health*. Sisters, OR: VMI Publishers, 2008.

Blomberg, Craig L. *The New American Commentary, Vol. 22, Matthew*. Edited by David S. Dockery. Nashville: B&H Publishing Group, 1992.

Borchert, Gerald L. *The New American Commentary, Vol. 25a, John 1-11*. Edited by E. Ray Clendenen. Nashville: B&H Publishing Group, 1996.

Borden, Paul D. *Hit the Bullseye*. Abingdon Press, Nashville. 2003.

Boschman, LaMar. *Future Worship*. Renew Books, Ventura, CA. 1999.

Bossidy, Larry, and Charan, Ram. *Execution*. New York: Crown Business, 2002.

Bowden, Boyce. "Different Paths to a Common Goal: Healthy, Revitalized Churches Making Disciples" *Interpreter Magazine Online* http://www.interpretermagazine.org/interior.asp?ptid=43&mid=11764 (assessed October 10, 2010).

Bowden, Andrew. *Ministry in the Countryside: A Model for the Future*. New York: Continuum Books, 2003.

Brady, Tom. "Missional Mergers: 9 keys to Success." *Outreach*, May/June, 2009.

Brown, Miriam Gen. Ed. *Sustaining Heart in the Heartland: Exploring Rural Spirituality*. New York: Paulist Press, 2005.

Brown, R. D., Truman Dale, and Robert D. Baker. *Reviving the Plateaued Church*. Nashville: Convention Press, 1991.

Bruce, F.F. *Commentary on the Book of Acts: The English Text with Introduction, Exposition and Notes*. Grand Rapids: Wm. B. Eerdmans Publishing Company, 1974.

Bruner, Frederick Dale. *Matthew, Vol. 2: The Churchbook Matthew 13-28*. Dallas: Word Publishing, 1990.

Brunson, Mac and Ergun Caner. *Why Churches Die: Diagnosing Lethal Poisons in the Body of Christ*. Nashville: B&H Publishing Group, 2005.

Bubna, Don. "Ten Reasons Not To Resign," *Leadership a Practical Journal for Church Leaders* Volume XXVI (Fall 2005): 74-80.

Bubna, Donald, Keith Walker and Jim VanYperen. "20 Questions to Determine Your Church's Health," *Leadership a Practical Journal for Church Leaders* Volume XVIII (Spring 1997): 41-42.

Bunker, Kerry A. and Michael Wakefield. *Leading with Authenticity in Times of Transition.* Greensboro, NC: Center for Creative Leadership Press, 2005.

Buttry, Daniel. *Bring Your Church Back to Life: Beyond Survival Mentality.* Valley Forge: Judson Press, 1988.

Callahan, Kennon L. *Effective Church Leadership: Building on the Twelve Keys.* San Francisco: Jossey-Bass, 1990.

Callahan, Kennon L. *Small, Strong Congregations: Creating Strengths and Health for Your Congregation.* San Francisco: Jossey-Bass, 2000.

Cameron, Kirt and Ray Comfort. *The School of Biblical Evangelism: 101 Lessons.* Alachua, FL: Bridge-Logos, 2004.

Cha, Peter S., Steve Kang, and Helen Lee. ed. *Growing Healthy Asian American Churches: Ministry Insights from Groundbreaking Congregations.* Downers Grove, IL: Inter Varsity Press, 2006.

Chadwick, William. *Stealing Sheep: The Church's Hidden Problem with Transfer Growth*. Downers Grove, IL: Inter Varsity Press, 2001.

Chambers, Andy. *Exemplary Life: A Theology of Church Life in Acts*. Nashville: B&H Publishing Group, 2012.

Cheyney, Tom and Jim Wigton, Church Revitalization & Renewal Podcast: Ingredients that are Necessary for a Church in Transition. (Https://blu177.mail.live.com) (accessed September 23, 2014).

Cheyney, Tom. *The Church Revitalizer as Change Agent*. Orlando: Renovate Publishing Group, 2016.

Cheyney, Tom. *Thirty-Eight Church Revitalization Models for the Twenty First Century*. Orlando: Renovate Publishing Group, 2014.

Cheyney, Tom. *The Seven Pillars of Church Revitalization and Renewal: The Biblical Foundation for Church Revitalization*. Orlando: Renovate Publishing Group, 2016.

Cheyney, Tom, and Terry Rials. *The Nuts and Bolts of Church Revitalization*. Orlando: Renovate Publishing Group, 2015.

Cheyney, Tom, David Putman, and Van Sanders. gen. eds. *Seven Steps for Planting Churches: Planter Edition*. Alpharetta, GA: North American Mission Board, 2003.

Cheyney, Tom and Larry Wynn. *Preaching Towards Church Revitalization and Renewal.* Orlando: Renovate Publishing Group, 2015.

Christy, Mark. *Breaking Numerical Barriers and Revitalizing Plateaued Churches.* Amazon Digital Services, Inc., 2012.

Clarensau, Michael H., Sylvia, Lee, and Steven R. Mills. *We Build People: Making Disciples for the 21st Century.* Springfield: Gospel Publishing House, 1998.

Clegg, Tom. *Missing in America: Making an Eternal Difference in the World Next Door.* Group, Loveland, Colorado. 2007.

Cole, Neil and Phil Helfer. *Church Transfusion: Changing Your Church Organically From the Inside Out.* San Francisco, CA: Josey-Bass, 2012.

Cole, Neil. *Organic Leadership: Leading Naturally Right Where You Are.* Grand Rapids: Baker Books, 2009.

Conner, Mark. *Transforming Your Church: Seven Strategic Shifts to Help You Successfully Navigate the 21st Century.* Tonbridge, Kent (England): Sovereign World, Ltd., 2000.

Conner, W.T. *Christian Doctrine.* Nashville: Broadman Press, 1937.

Coote, Robert B. Gen. Ed. *Mustard-Seed Churches: Ministries in Small Churches*. Minneapolis: Fortress Press, 1990.

Coppedge, Anthony D. *The Reason Your Church Must Twitter: Making Your Ministry Contagious. E-book 2008*. http://twitterforchurches.com (accessed 10/26/2010).

Cordeiro, Wayne. *Doing Church as a Team: The Miracle of Teamwork and How it Transforms Churches*. Ventura: Regal Books, 2001.

Cordeiro, Wayne. *Leading on Empty: Refilling Your Tank and Renewing Your Passion*. Minneapolis: Bethany House Publishers, 2010.

Crandall, Ron. *Turnaround and Beyond: A Hopeful Future for Small Membership Churches*. Nashville: Abingdon Press, 2008. (rev. ed. of Turnaround Strategies for the Small Church. c 1995).

Crandall, Ron. *Turn Around Strategies for the Small Church*. Nashville: Abingdon Press, 1995.

Creps, Earl G., *Off-road Disciplines: Spiritual Adventures of Missional Leaders*. 1st ed. San Francisco: Jossey-Bass, 2006.

Creps, Earl G. *Reverse Mentoring: How Young Leaders Can Transform the Church and Why We Should Let Them*. San Francisco: Jossey-Bass, 2008.

Crow, Charles D. & Crow, Kenneth E. "The Church Growth Movement and the American Dream," *Grow Magazine*. Bethany, OK: Church of the Nazarene, 2003. Download at: www.nazarene.org

Dale, Robert D. *Leadership for a Changing Church: Charting the Shape of the River*. Nashville: Abingdon Press, 1998.

Dale, Robert. *To Dream Again: How to Help Your Church Come Alive*. Nashville: Broadman Press, 1983.

Davis, Ronald L. *The Revitalization of The African-American Baptist Church, Association and Convention: Addressing Organizational Structures, Pastoral Leadership, Racial Reconciliation, and Socio-Economic Issues*. Maitland, FL: Xulon Press, 2014.

Dever, Mark. *Nine Marks of a Healthy Church*. Wheaton: Crossway Books, 2000.

Dever, Mark. *What is a Healthy Church?* Wheaton: Crossway Books, 2007.

Devine, Mark and Darrin Patrick. Replant: How a Dying Church Can Grow Again. David C. Cook, 2014.

DeYmaz, Mark. *Building a Healthy Multi-ethnic Church: Mandate, Commitments and Practices of a Diverse Congregation*. San Francisco: Jossey-Bass, 2007.

Dockery, David S., Ray Van Neste, and Jerry Tidwell, *Southern Baptists, Evangelicals and the Future of Denominationalism.* Nashville: B&H Publishing Group, 2011.

Dudley, Carl S. *Making the Small Church Effective.* Nashville: Abingdon Press, 1993.

Dudley, Carl S, and Sally A. Johnson. *Energizing the Congregation: Images That Shape Your Church's Ministry.* Louisville: Westminster John Knox Press, 1993.

Duin, Julia. *Quitting Church: Why the Faithful Are Fleeing and What to Do About It.* Grand Rapids: Baker Books, 2008.

Dunagin, Richard L., and Lyle E. Schaller. *Beyond These Walls: Building the Church in a Built-out Neighborhood.* Nashville: Abingdon Press. 1999.

Dunn, James D.G. *The Acts of the Apostles.* Valley Forge, PA: Trinity Press International, 1996.

Earman, Jeffrey M. *Resuscitating the Almost Dead: Breathing New Life Into Your Church.* CreateSpace Independent Publishing, 2013.

Erickson, Millard J. *Christian Theology.* Grand Rapids: Baker Book House, 1985.

Ezell, Kevin and Larry Wynn, North American Mission Board Podcast: Church Revitalization. http://www.namb.net/podcast-church-revtalization/(accessed September 29, 2014).

Falwell, Jonathan. General ed. *Innovatechurch: Innovative Leadership for the Next Generation Church.* Nashville: B&H Publishing Group, 2008.

Faulkner, Brooks R. *Burnout in Ministry: How to Recognize It, How to Avoid It.* Nashville: Broadman Press, 1981.

Fee, Gordon D. *The First Epistle to the Corinthians.* Grand Rapids: Wm. B. Eerdmans Publishing Company, 1987.

Fensham, F.C. *The Books of Ezra and Nehemiah*, NICOT., Grand Rapids: Eerdmans, 1982.

Finke, Roger, and Rodney Stark. *The Churching of America 1776 – 2005: Winners and Losers in Our Religious Economy.* New Brunswick, New Jersey: Rutgers University Press, 2008.

Fletcher, Michael. *Overcoming Barriers to Growth: Proven Strategies for Taking Your Church to the Next Level.* Ada, MI: Bethany House, 2009.

Foster, Richard J. *Celebration of Discipline.* San Francisco: Harper Collins Publishers, 1998.

Foss, Michael F. Preaching for Revitalization. Christian Focus Publications, Ltd: Geanies House, Fearn, Ross-Shire, Scotland, 2006.

Fowler, Harry H. *Breaking Barriers of New Church Growth: Increasing Attendance from 0-150*. Rocky Mount, NC: Creative Growth Dynamics, Inc., 1988.

Frank, Dottie Escobedo. *Restart Your Church*. Nashville: Abingdon Press, 2012.

Frazee, Randy. *The Connecting Church: Beyond Small Groups to Authentic Community*. Grand Rapids, MI: Zondervan, 2001.

Friedman, Edwin H. *A Failure of Nerve: Leadership in the Age of the Quick Fix*. New York: Seabury Books, 2007.

Fuder, John. *Neighborhood Mapping: How to Make Your Church Invaluable to the Community*. Chicago: Moody Publishers, 2014.

Geldenhuys, Norval. *Commentary on the Gospel of Luke: The English Text with Introduction Exposition and Notes*. Grand Rapids: Wm. B. Eerdmans Publishing Company, 1975.

George, Carl F. *Beyond 800: Transitioning for Greater Impact*. Diamond Bar, CA: MetaChurch Publishing, 1995.

George, Carl. *Beyond 400: Transitioning for Greater Impact.* Diamond Bar, CA: MetaChurch Publishing, 1995.

George, Carl F. with C. Peter Wagner. *Beyond 200.* Diamond Bar, CA: MetaChurch Publishing, 1995.

George, Carl F. with Warren Bird. *How to Break Growth Barriers: Capturing Overlooked Opportunities for Church Growth.* Grand Rapids: Baker Book House, 1993.

Gerber, Michael. *E-Myth Revisited.* New York: Harper Collins Publishers, 1995.

Getz, Gene, and Joe Wall. *Effective Church Growth Strategies.* Nashville: Thomas Nelson Publishers, 2000.

Getz, Gene A. *The Measure of a Healthy Church.* Chicago: Moody Publishers, 2007.

Gibbs, Eddie. *ChurchNext: Quantum Changes in How We Do Ministry.* Downers Grove, IL: InterVarsity Press, 2000.

Gleason, Michael. *Building on Living Stones: New Testament Patterns and Principles of Renewal.* Grand Rapids: Kregel Academic Publications, 1996.

Godin, Seth. *The Dip: A Little Book that Teaches You When to Quit and When to Stick.* New York: Penguin Group, 2007.

Green, Matthew. "Megachurch Myths." *MinistryToday Magazine*, http://www.ministrytodaymag.com/index.php/features/12951-megachurch-myths May/June 2006, 46-47.

Green, Michael. *Thirty Years that Changed the World: The Book of Acts for Today*. Grand Rapids: William B. Eerdmans Publishing Company, 2002.

Groeschel, Craig. *It: How Churches and Leaders Can Get It and Keep It*. Grand Rapids: Zondervan, 2008.

"Growing Small and Medium Churches." *Journal of Evangelism and Missions*. Volume 9 (Spring 2010): Cordova, TN and Schenectady, NY: 2010.

Hadaway, C. Kirk. *Church Growth Principles*. Nashville: Broadman Press, 1991.

Halter, Hugh, and Matt Smay. *AND: The Gathered and Scattered Church*. Grand Rapids: Zondervan, 2010.

Hammett, Edward H. with James R. Pierce. *Reaching People Under 40 While Keeping People Over 60*. St. Louis, MO: Chalice Press, 2007.

Hammond, Thomas, and Steve Wilkes. "Church Conflict/Church Growth," *Journal of Evangelism and Missions* Volume Seven (Spring 2008): 3-11.

Harding, Kevass J. *Can These Bones Live: Bringing New Life to a Dying Church?* Nashville: Abingdon Press, 2007.

Harney, Kevin G. and Bob Bouwer. *The U-Turn Church: New Direction for Health and Growth.* Grand Rapids: Baker Books, 2011.

Harris, Joshua. *Stop Dating the Church: Fall in Love with the Family of God.* Colorado Springs: Multnomah Publishers, 2004.

Harrison, Rodney. *Seven Steps for Planting Churches: Partnering Churches Edition.* Alpharetta, GA: North American Mission Board, 2004.

Harrison, Rodney, Tom Cheyney, and Don Overstreet. *SPIN-OFF CHURCHES: How One Church Successfully Plants Another.* Nashville: B&H Publishing Group, 2008.

Hassinger, Edward W., John S. Holik, and J. Kenneth Benson. *The Rural Church: Learning from Three Decades of Change.* Nashville: Abingdon Press, 1988.

Hawkins, O.S. *Rebuilding: It's Never Too Late for a New Beginning.* Dallas: Annuity Board of the Southern Baptist Convention, 1999.

Hays, Richard B. *First Corinthians: A Bible Commentary for Teaching and Preaching.* Louisville: John Knox Press, 1997.

Hazelton, Paul N. *7 Steps to Revitalizing the Small-Town Church*. Kansas City: Beacon Hill Press, 1993.

Hellerman, Joseph H. *When the Church was the Family: Recapturing Jesus' Vision for Authentic Christian Community*. Nashville, TN: B&H Publishing Group, 2009.

Hemphill, Ken. *The Antioch Effect: 8 Characteristics of Highly Effective Churches*. Nashville: Broadman & Holman Publishers, 1994.

Hemphill, Ken. *The Bonsai Theory of Church Growth*. Nashville: Broadman Press, 1991.

Hemphill, Ken and Mike James. *Velcro Church*. Nashville: Auxano Press, 2013.

Hendricks, William D. *Exit Interviews: Revealing Stories of Why People Are Leaving the Church*. Chicago: Moody Press, 1993.

Hendriksen, William. *New Testament Commentary: Exposition of the Gospel According to Mark*. Grand Rapids: Baker Books, 1975.

Hendriksen, William. *New Testament Commentary: Exposition of the Gospel According to Matthew*. Grand Rapids: Baker Academic, 1973.

Hendriksen, William. *New Testament Commentary: Exposition of the Gospel According to Luke*. Grand Rapids: Baker Academic, 1978.

Herrington, Jim, Mike Bonem, and James H. Furr. *Leading Congregational Change: A Practical Guide for the Transformational Journey.* San Francisco: Jossey-Bass, 2000.

Hirsch, Alan and Tim Catchim. *The Permanent Revolution: Apostolic Imagination and Practice for the 21st Century Church.* San Francisco: Jossey-Bass, 2012.

Hoeft, Jeanne, L. Shannon Jung and Joretta Marshall. *Practicing Care in Rural Congregations and Communities.* Minneapolis: Fortress Press, 2013.

Holt, William R. *Effectiveness By the Numbers: Counting What Counts in the Church.* Nashville: Abingdon Press, 2007.

Hood, Pat. *The Sending Church: The Church Must Leave the Building.* Nashville: B&H Books, 2013.

House, Polly. "Small Churches Go Transformational" http:www.bpnews.net/bpnews.asp?Id=33765 (assessed September 28, 2010).

Howell Jr., Don N. *Servant of the Servant: A Biblical Theology of Leadership.* Eugene, OR: Wipf & Stock Publishers, 2003.

Hudnall, Todd. *Church, Come Forth: A Biblical Plan for Transformational Turnaround.* Nashville: CrossBooks, 2014.

Hull, Bill. *Seven Steps to Transform Your Church*. Grand Rapids: Fleming H. Revell, 1993.

Hull, Bill. *The Disciple-Making Pastor: The Key to Building Healthy Christians in Today's Church*. Grand Rapids: Fleming H. Revell, 1988.

Hunt, Josh, *Change Your Church or Die*. CreateSpace Independent Publishing, 2014. Hunter, Kent R. *The Lord's Harvest and the Rural Church: A New Look at Ministry in the Agri-Culture*. Kansas City: Beacon Hill Press of Kansas City, 1993.

Irwin, L. Gail. *Toward the Better Country: Church Closure and Resurrection*. Eugene, OR: Resource Publications, 2014.

Iorg, Jeff. *The Painful Side of Leadership: Moving Forward Even When It Hurts*. Nashville: B&H Publishing Group. 2009.

Jackson, Anne. *Mad Church Disease: Overcoming the Burnout Epidemic*. Grand Rapids: Zondervan, 2009.

Johnson, Alan F. "Revelation." In *The Expositor's Bible Commentary*, vol. 12, edited by Frank E. Gaebelein. Grand Rapids: Baker Books, 2004.

Johnson, Heather, and Lindy Lowry. "25 Ideas & Trends Reshaping the American Church," *Outreach*, January/February, 2009.

Jones, Peyton. *Church Zero: Raising 1st Century Churches out of the Ashes of the 21st Century Church*. David C. Cook, 2013.

Jung, L. Shannon and Mary A. Agris. *Rural Congregational Studies: A Guide for Good Shepherds*. Nashville: Abingdon, 1997.

Keenan, Tracy. "Finding the Focal Point," *Leadership a Practical Journal for Church Leaders* Volume XVIII (Spring 1997): 35-36.

Keener, Ronald E. "Pulling Back from the Brink," *Church Executive*, November, 2008. Kidner, Derek. *Psalms 1-72 and Psalms 73-150 Two Volumes*, Tyndale Old Testament Commentary. Grand Rapids: Eerdmans, 1973.

Kimball, Dan. *They Like Jesus But Not the Church: Insights from Emerging Generations*. Zondervan, Grand Rapids, MI. 2007.

Kistemaker, Simon J. *Revelation*. New Testament Commentary. Grand Rapids: Baker Books, 2004.

Klassen, Ronald and John Koessler. *No Little Places: The Untapped Potential of the Small-Town Church*. Grand Rapids: Baker Books, 2002.

Kneisel, Harvey. *New Life for Declining Churches: New Hope, New Vision, New Strategy, New Life!* Houston: Macedonian Call Foundation, 1995.

Kotter, John P. *Leading Change.* Boston: Harvard Business School Press, 1996.

Küng, Hans. *The Church.* Garden City, NY: Image Books, 1976.

Lancaster, Lynne C. and David Stillman. *The M-factor: How the Millennial Generation is Rocking the Workplace.* New York: HarperCollins Publishers, 2010.

Lane, William L. *The Gospel According to Mark: The English Text with Introduction, Exposition and Notes.* Grand Rapids: Wm. B. Eerdmans Publishing Company, 1974.

Laubach, David C. *12 Steps to Congregational Transformation.* Valley Forge: Judson Press, 2006.

Lawless, Chuck. *Discipled Warriors: Growing Healthy Churches That Are Equipped for Spiritual Warfare.* Grand Rapids: Kregel Academic, 2002.

Lee, James D. *How to Kill a Church in One Year or Less: Guaranteed: Twelve Easy Steps to Preventing Church Growth.* Lexington, KY: 2004.

Leeman, Jonathan. *Church Membership: How the World Knows Who Represents Jesus.* Wheaton, IL: Crossway, 2012.

Logan, Robert E. *Beyond Church Growth: Action Plans for Developing a Dynamic Church.* Grand Rapids: Fleming H. Revell, 1990.

Longenecker, Harold L. *Building Town and Country Churches: A Practical Approach to the Revitalization of Churches.* Chicago: Moody Press, 1973.

Longenecker, Richard N. *The Expositor's Bible Commentary, Volume 9, John-Acts.* Edited by Frank E. Gaebelein. Grand Rapids: Zondervan Publishing House, 1981.

Macchia, Stephen A. *Becoming a Healthy Church: 10 Characteristics.* Grand Rapids: Baker Books, 1999.

Macchia, Stephen. "Health Checkup: Ten Telltale Signs of Church Health" *Leadership a Practical Journal for Church Leaders* Volume XVIII (Spring 1997): 36.

MacDonald, Gordon. *Who Stole My Church: What to Do When the Church You Love Tries to Enter the Twenty-first Century* Nashville: Thomas Nelson, 2007.

Malphurs, Aubrey. *Advanced Strategic Planning: A New Model for Church and Ministry Leaders.* 2nd. ed. Grand Rapids: Baker Books, 2005.

Malphurs, Aubrey. *Pouring New Wine into Old Wineskins: How Change a Church without Destroying It.* Grand Rapids: Baker Publishing Group, 1993.

Mann, Alice. *Can Our Church Live: Redeveloping Congregations in Decline*. Herndon, Virginia: The Alban Institute, 1999.

Marshall, Howard I. *Acts of the Apostles: An Introduction and Commentary*. Grand Rapids: Wm.

Martin, Kevin E. *Myth of the 200 Barrier: How to Lead Through Transitional Growth*. Nashville: Abingdon Press, 2005.

Marquart, Kurt E. "Some Aspects of a Healthy Church Life." Lutheran Theological Journal 3, no. 1 (May 1, 1969): 14-135. ATLA Religion Database with ATLASerials, EBSCOhost (accessed February 2, 2010).

McCarty, Doran. *Leading the Small Church*. Nashville: Broadman Press, 1991. McConnell, Scott. *Multi-site Churches: Guidance for the Movement's Next Generation*. Nashville: B&H Publishing Group, 2009.

McConnell, William T. *Renew Your Congregation: Healing the Sick, Raising the Dead*. St. Louis: Chalice Press, 2007.

McCutcheon, Michael. *Rebuilding God's People: Strategies for Revitalizing Declining Churches*. Camp Hill, PA: Christian Publications, 1993.

McGavran, Donald A., and Peter C. Wagner. *Understanding Church Growth*. Grand Rapids: Wm. B. Eerdmans Publishing Co., 1990.

McGavran, Donald Anderson, and Win Arn. *Ten Steps for Church Growth*. 1st ed. San Francisco: HarperCollins Publishers, 1977.

McIntosh, Gary L. "A Critique of the Critics," *Journal of Evangelism and Missions* Volume Two (Spring 2003): 37-50.

McIntosh, Gary L. *Beyond the First Visit: The Complete Guide to Connecting Guests to Your Church*. Grand Rapids, MI: Baker Books, 2006.

McIntosh, Gary L. *Here Today, There Tomorrow: Unleashing Your Church's Potential*. Indianapolis, IN: Wesleyan Publishing House, 2010.

McIntosh, Gary. *One Size Doesn't Fit All: Bringing Out the Best in Any Size Church*. Grand Rapids: Fleming H. Revell, 1999.

McIntosh, Gary. *Staff Your Church for Growth: Building Team Ministry in the 21st Century*. Grand Rapids: Baker Books, 2002.

McIntosh, Gary. *Taking Your Church to the Next Level: What Got You Here Won't Get You There*. Grand Rapids: Baker Books, 2009.

McIntosh, Gary, and Robert L. Edmonson. *It Only Hurts on Monday: Why Pastors Quit and What You Can Do about It*. Carol Stream, IL: ChurchSmart Resources, 1998.

McMullen, Shawn, and Mary Elizabeth Hopkins. "Common Size, Uncommon Impact," *Outreach*, July/August, 2006.

McMullen, Shawn. ed. *Releasing the Power of the Smaller Church*. Cincinnati, OH: Standard Publishing. 2007.

McMullen, Shawn. ed. *Unleashing the Potential of the Smaller Church: Vision and Strategy for Life- Changing Ministry*. Cincinnati, OH: Standard Publishing. 2006.

McNeal, Reggie. *The Present Future: Six Tough Questions for the Church*. San Francisco: Jossey Bass, 2003.

Miles, David. *ReTurn Resource Kit: Restoring Churches to the Heart of God*. Carol Stream, IL: ChurchSmart Resources, 2005.

Miller, C. John. *Outgrowing the Ingrown Church*. Grand Rapids: Zondervan Publishing House, 1986.

Miller, Kevin A. "Church Health: Developing a Vital Ministry." Leadership 18, no. 3 (June 1, 1997): 21. ATLA Religion Database with ATLASerials, EBSCOhost (accessed February 2, 2010).

Moore, W. Scott. *Rural Pastor's Handbook: A How To Guide for Leading Your Flock*. Rogersville, AL: Eleos Press, 2014.

Moore, W. Scott. Rural Revival: Growing Churches in Shrinking Communities. Rogersville, AL: Eleos Press, 2012.

Munton, Doug. *Seven Steps to Becoming a Healthy Christian Leader.* Sisters, OR: VMI Publishers, 2004.

Murray, Stuart. 2001. *Church Planting: Laying Foundations* Scottsdale, PN: Herald Press, 2001.

Murrow, David. *Why Men Hate Going to Church*. Nashville: Thomas Nelson Books, 2005.

Myers, Gary. "Stetzer Highlights Keys to Church Revitalization," http:www.baptistcourier.com/2057.article (assessed October 10, 2010).

Neighbor, Jr., Ralph W. "It's the Structure, Period," *Leadership a Practical Journal for Church Leaders* Volume XVIII (Spring 1997): 36-37.

Nixon, David F. *Leading the Comeback Church: Help Your Church Rebound from Decline*. Kansas City, MO: Beacon Hill Press, 2004.

Nixon, Paul. *I Refuse to Lead a Dying Church*. Cleveland, OH: The Pilgrim Press, 2006.

Oaks, Fred. "Renewing Older Churches," *Leadership a Practical Journal for Church Leaders* Volume XXVI (Fall 2005): 47-49.

Ogden, Greg. *The New Reformation: Returning the Ministry to the People of God.* Grand Rapids: Zondervan Publishing House, 1992.

Ogne, Steve and Tim Roehl. *TransforMissional Coaching: Empowering Leaders in a Changing Ministry World.* B&H Publishing Group, Nashville, TN. 2008.

Oldenburg, Ray. Editor. *Celebrating the Third Place: Inspiring Stories about the "Great Good Places" at the Heart of Our Communities.* Harlowe & Company, New York. 2001.

Olson, David T. *The American Church in Crisis.* Grand Rapids: Zondervan, 2008.

O'Malley, J. Steven. *Interpretive Trends in Christian Revitalization for the Early Twenty First Century.* Emeth Press, 2011.

Ortlund, Anne and Ray Ortlund. *You Don't Have to Quit: How to Persevere When You Want to Give Up!* Nashville: Thomas Nelson Publishers, 1994.

Ott, E. Stanley. *Twelve Dynamic Shifts for Transforming Your Church.* Grand Rapids: William B. Eerdmans Publishing Company, 2002.

Owen, Marvin. "25 Signs of a Healthy Church" *Deacon*, Spring 2008.

Packer, J.I. *Taking God Seriously: Vital Things We Need to Know.* Wheaton, IL: Crossway, 2013

Page, Frank with John Perry. *Who Can Save the Incredible Shrinking Church?* Nashville: B&H Publishing Group, 2008.

Partner, Daniel. Ed. *The Essential Works of Charles Spurgeon: Selected Books, Sermons, and Other Writings.* Uhrichsville, OH: Barbour Publishing, Inc., 2009,

Patton, Jeff. *If It Could Happen Here: Turning the Small-Membership Church Around.* Nashville: Abingdon, 2002.

Pearle, Bob. *The Vanishing Church: Searching for Significance in the 21st Century.* Garland, TX: Hannibal Books, 2009.

Perman, Matthew. *What's Bet Next: How the Gospel Transforms the Way You Get Things Done.* Grand Rapids: Zondervan, 2014.

Pierson, Robert D. *Needs-based Evangelism: Being a Good Samaritan Church.* Nashville: Abingdon Press, 2006.

Powell, Paul W. *Shepherding the Sheep in Smaller Churches. Dallas:* Annuity Board of the Southern Baptist Convention, 1995.

Preston, Gary. *Pastors in Pain: How to Grow in Times of Conflict.* Grand Rapids: Baker Books, 1999.

Quicke, Michael J. *360 Degree Preaching.* Baker Academic, Grand Rapids, MI. 2003. Quinn, Robert E. *Deep Change: Discovering the Leader Within.* San Francisco: Jossey Bass, 1996.

Rainer, Thom. *Autopsy of a Deceased Church: 12 Ways to Keep Yours Alive.* Nashville: B&H Publishing Group, 2014.

Rainer, Thom. "Five Major Trends for Churches in America" http://www.churchcentral.com/blog/Five-major-trends-for-churches-in-America (assessed October 6, 2010).

Rainer, Thom S. *Breakout Churches: Discover How to Make the Leap.* Grand Rapids: Zondervan, 2005.

Rainer, Thom S. *High Expectations: the Remarkable Secret for Keeping People in Your Church.* Nashville: B&H Publishing Group, 1999.

Rainer, Thom S. *Seven Reasons Why We Should Not Give Up on Established Churches.* (Https://ThomRainer.com/podcast-2/) (accessed September 23, 2014).

Rainer, Thom S. "Seven Sins of Dying Churches," *Outreach,* November/December, 2005.

Rainer, Thom S. "Seven Sins of Dying Churches," *Outreach*, January/February, 2006.

Rainer, Thom S. *Surprising Insights from the Unchurched and Proven Ways to Reach Them*. Grand Rapids: Zondervan, 2008.

Rainer, Thom S. *The Unchurched Next Door: Understanding Faith Stages as Keys to Sharing Your Faith*. Grand Rapids: Zondervan, 2003.

Rainer, Thom S. *Vibrant Church: Becoming a Healthy Church in the 21st Century*. Nashville, TN: LifeWay Press, 2008.

Rainer, Thom S. and Daniel L. Akin. *Vibrant Church: Becoming a Healthy Church in the 21st Century*. Nashville: Lifeway Press, 2008.

Rainer, Tom and Eric, Geiger. *Simple Church: Returning to God's Process for Making Disciples*. Nashville: Broadman & Holman Publishing, 2006.

Rainer, Thom S. and Sam S. Rainer III. "Coming Home," *Outreach*, July/August, 2007.

Rainer, Thom S. and Sam S. Rainer III. "Reaching the "Hardcore" Unchurched," *Outreach*, November/December, 2008.

Rainer, Thom S. and Sam S. Rainer. "The Essential Church Expects More," *Outreach*, July/August, 2006.

Reeder III, Harry L. with David Swavely. *From Embers to a Flame: How to Revitalize Your Church*. Revised and Expanded Ed., Phillipsburg, NJ: P&R Publishing Company, 2008.

Reeves, Thomas C. *The Empty Church: Does Organized Religion Matter Anymore?* New York: Touchstone, 1996.

Regele, Mike, with Mark Schultz. *Death of the Church*. Grand Rapids: Zondervan Publishing House, 1995.

Reid, Alvin L. REVITALIZE Your Church Through Gospel Recovery. Gospel Advance Books, 2013.

Ricketson, Rusty. *Follower First: Rethinking Leading in the Church*. Cumming, GA: Heartworks Publications, 2009.

Riley, Linda. "When Your Wife Resents Your Call," *Leadership a Practical Journal for Church Leaders* Volume XXVI (Fall 2005): 51-55.

Rizzo, Dino. *Servolution: Starting a Church Revolution Through Serving*. Zondervan, Grand Rapids, MI. 2009.

Robertson, Paul E. "Theology for the Healthy Church." *Theological Educator: A Journal of Theology and Ministry* no. 57 (March 1, 1998): 45. ATLA Religion Database with ATLASerials, EBSCOhost (accessed February 2, 2010).

Ross, Michael F. *Preaching for Revitalization: How to Revitalize Your Church Through Your Pulpit.* San Francisco, CA: Mentor Imprint, 2006.

Roxburgh, Alan J. and Fred Romanuk. *The Missional Leader: Equipping Your Church to Reach a Changing World.* Jossey-Bass, San Francisco, CA. 2006.

Ruffcorn, Kevin E. *Rural Evangelism: Catching the Vision.* Minneapolis: Augsburg Fortress, 1994.

Ruffle, Douglas W. *Roadmap to Renewal: Rediscovering the Church's Mission.* New York: The General Board of Global Ministries, The United Methodist Church, 2009.

Russell, Ronny. *Can a Church Live Again?: The Revitalization of a 21st Century Church.* Macon, GA: Smyth & Helwys Publishing, 2004.

Ryle, J.C. *Mark: Expository Thoughts on the Gospels.* Edited by A. McGrath and J.I. Packer, Wheaton, IL: Crossway Books, 1993.

Scazzero, Peter. *Emotionally Healthy Spirituality.* Integrity, Franklin, TN. 2006.

Schaller, Lyle E. *Activating the Passive Church: Diagnosis & Treatment.* Nashville: Abingdon Press, 1982. (Out of print but can be found at Amazon.com)

Schaller, Lyle E. *44 Questions for Congregational Self-appraisal.* Nashville: Abingdon Press. 1998.

Schaller, Lyle E. *44 Steps Up Off the Plateau.* Nashville: Abingdon Press, 1993.

Schaller, Lyle E. *44 Ways to Increase Church Attendance.* Nashville: Abingdon Press, 1988.

Schaller, Lyle E. *Small Congregation, Big Potential: Ministry in the Small Membership Church.* Nashville: Abingdon Press. 2003.

Schnase, Robert. *Five Practices of Fruitful Congregations.* Nashville: Abingdon Press, 2007.

Schwarz, Christian A. *Natural Church Development: A Guide to Eight Essential Qualities of Healthy Churches.* Carol Stream, IL: ChurchSmart Resources, 1996.

Scott, Marvin. *25 Reasons Why Small Churches Aren't Growing.* Longwood, FL: Xulon Press, 2006.

Searcy, Nelson and Jennifer Dykes Henson. *Ignite: How to Spark Immediate Growth in Your Church.* Grand Rapids: Baker Books, 2009.

Sellon, Mary K., Daniel P. Smith and Gail F. Grossman. *Redeveloping the Congregation.* Herndon, VA: Alban Institute, 2002.

Shanks, Carol. *Choosing To Be A "What If" Church: One Church's Story of Revitalization.* CreateSpace Independent Publishing Platform, 2011.

Shelley, Marshall. "Double-Digit Churches," *Leadership a Practical Journal for Church Leaders* Volume IV (Fall 1983): 38-49.

Sjogren, Steve. *101 Ways to Reach Your Community.* Colorado Springs: NavPress, 2001.

Slaughter, Michael. *Spiritual Entrepreneurs: 6 Principles for Risky Renewal.* Nashville: Abingdon Press, 1996.

Smith, Daniel P. and Mary K. Sellon. *Pathway to Renewal: Practical Steps for Congregations*, Herndon, Virginia: The Alban Institute, 2008.

Smith, Ebbie. *Growing Healthy Churches: New Directions for Church Growth in the 21st Century*, Dallas: Church Starting Network, 2003.

Smith, Efrem, and Phil Jackson. *The Hip-hop Church: Connecting with the Movement Shaping Our Culture.* Downers Grove, IL: InterVarsity Press. 2006.

Smith, Rockwell C. *Rural Ministry and the Changing Community.* Nashville: Abingdon Press, 1971.

Southerland, Dan. *Transitioning: Leading Your Church through Change*. Grand Rapids: Zondervan, 1999.

Spader, Dan, and Gary Mayes. *Growing a Healthy Church*. Chicago: Moody Press, 1991.

Spader, and Gary Mayes. "Growing a Healthy Church," *Leadership a Practical Journal for Church Leaders* Volume XVIII (Spring 1997): 38.

Spurgeon, Rev. C. H. *Sermons of the Rev. C. H. Spurgeon of London*, New York: Sheldon Blakeman and Company, 1857.

Stanley, Andy. *Visioneering*. Sisters, OR: Multnomah Publishers, 1999.

Steinke, Peter L. *Congregational Leadership in Anxious Times: Being Calm and Courageous No Matter What*. Herndon, VA: The Alban Institute, 2006.

Stetzer, Ed and David Putman. *Breaking the Missional Code: Your Church Can Become a Missionary in Your Community*. Nashville: B&H Publishing Group, 2006.

Stetzer, Ed, and Mike Dodson. *Comeback Churches: How 300 Churches Turned Around and Yours Can Too*. Nashville: B. & H. Publishers, 2007.

Stetzer, Ed and Thomas S. Rainer. *Transformational Church: Creating a New Scorecard for Congregations*. Nashville: B&H Publishing Group, 2010.

Stone, Charles. *Ministry Killers and How to Defeat Them: Help for Frustrated Pastors* Minneapolis: Bethany House Publishers, 2010.

Strachan, Owen and Kyle Idleman. *Risky Gospel: Abandon Fear and Build Something Awesome*. Nashville: Thomas Nelson, 2013.

Stein, Robert H. *Mark: Baker Exegetical Commentary on the New Testament*. Grand Rapids: Baker Academic, 2008.

Stein, Robert H. *The New American Commentary, Vol. 24, Luke*. Edited by David S. Dockery. Nashville: B&H Publishing Group, 1992.

Steinke, Peter L. *Congregational Leadership in Anxious Times: Being Calm and Courageous No Matter What*. Herndon, VA: Alban Institute, 2006.

Surratt, Geoff. *Ten Stupid Things That Keep Churches from Growing: How Leaders Can Overcome Costly Mistakes*. Grand Rapids: Zondervan, 2009.

Suirratt, Geoff, Greg Ligon, and Warren Bird. *A Multi-Site Church Road Trip: Exploring the New Normal*. Grand Rapids: Zondervan, 2009.

Suiratt, Geoff, Greg Ligon, and Warren Bird. *The Multi-Site Church Revolution: Being One Church in Many Locations.* Grand Rapids: Zondervan, 2006.

Sullivan, Bill. *New Perspectives on Breaking the 200 Barrier.* Kansas City: Beacon Hill Press, 2005.

Sullivan, Bill M. *Ten Steps to Breaking the 200 Barrier.* Kansas City: Beacon Hill Press, 1988.

Swindoll, Charles R. *The Church Awakening: An Urgent Call for Renewal.* New York: FaithWords, 2010.

Tenney, Merrill C. *John the Gospel of Belief: An Analytic Study of the Text.* Grand Rapids: William B. Eerdmans Publishing Company, 1948.

Terry, John Mark. *Church Evangelism: Creating a Culture for Growth in Your Congregation.* Nashville: Broadman & Holman Publishers, 1997.

Thiselton, Anthony C. *First Corinthians: A Shorter Exegetical and Pastoral Commentary.* Grand Rapids: Wm. B. Eerdmans Publishing Company, 2006.

Thorstad, Brian A. *Heaven Help Our Church: A Step-By-Step Survival Guide for Christians in Troubled Churches.* Minneapolis: NextStep Resources, 2013.

Thrasher, Kenneth C. *The Complex Ministry of Rural Church Pastors.* Chattanooga: AMG Publishers, 1984.

Thumma, Scotty. Travis, Dave. *Beyond Megachurch Myths: What We Can Learn from America's Largest Churches.* San Francisco: Jossey-Bass, 2007.

Thumma, Scott and Warren Bird. *The Other 80 Percent: Turning Your Church's Spectators into Active Participants.* Sisters, OR: Jossey-Bass, 2011.

Towns, Elmer L. "The Beginning of the Church Growth Movement," *Journal of Evangelism and Missions* Volume Two (Spring 2003): 13-19.

Tucker, Sonny. "The Fragmentation of the Post-McGavran Church Growth Movement," *Journal of Evangelism and Missions* Volume Two (Spring 2003): 21-35.

Turner, Emil. "Some Observations on "Church Splits" in the Arkansas Baptist State Convention," *Journal of Evangelism and Missions* Volume Seven (Spring 2008): 27-35.

Vannoy, Karen and John Flowers. *10 Temptations of Church: Why Churches Decline and What To Do About It.* Abingdon Press, 2012.

Viola, Frank and George Barna. *Pagan Christianity: Exploring the Roots of Our Church Practices.* Tyndale House Publishers, 2002.

Wagner, C. Peter. *Strategies for Church Growth: Tools for Effective Mission and Evangelism.* Ventura, CA: Regal Books, 1989.

Wagner, C. Peter. *The Healthy Church.* Ventura: Regal Books, 1996.

Walrath, Douglas Alan. *Leading Churches through Change.* Nashville: Abingdon Press, 1979.

Warren, Rick. "FIRST PERSON: Forget church growth, aim for church health." *Baptist Press* http://www.bpnews.net/bpnews.asp?id=13131 (accessed October 15, 2010).

Washington, Rev. Dr. John Edward. *The Church Stimulus Package: Jump Start Your Ministry and Revitalize Your Church.* Bloomington, IN: AuthorHouse, 2010.

Wells, Barney, Martin Giese, and Ron Klassen. *Leading Through Change: Shepherding the Town and Country Church in a New Era.* St. Charles, IL: ChurchSmart Resources, 2005.

Werning, Waldo J. *12 Pillars of a Healthy Church.* St. Charles, IL: ChurchSmart, 2001.

Westbury, Joe, Managing Editor. The Christian Index website. "Have Southern Baptists Joined the Evangelical Decline?"

http://www.christianindex.org/4421.article. Published May 22, 2008. (accessed September 29, 2014).

"What Does a Healthy Church Look Like?" *Leadership a Practical Journal for Church Leaders* Volume XVIII (Spring 1997): 34-35.

White, James Emery. *Rethinking the Church: A Challenge to Creative Resign in an Age of Transition.* Grand Rapids: Baker Books, 1997.

White, Michael and Tom Corcoran. *Rebuilt: Awakening the Faithful, Reaching the Lost, and Making Church Matter.* Ave Maria Press, 2013.

White, Thomas, Jason G. Duesing, and Malcolm B. Yarnell III, eds. *Restoring Integrity in Baptist Churches.* Grand Rapids: Kregel Publications, 2008.

Whitesel, Bob. *Growth by Accident, Death by Planning: How Not to Kill a Growing Congregation.* Nashville: Abingdon Press, 2004.

Whitesel, Bob. *The Healthy Church: Practical Ways to Strengthen a Church's Heart.* Indianapolis: Wesleyan Publishing House, 2013.

Whitesel. *Organix: Signs of Leadership in a Changing Church.* Nashville: Abingdon Press, 2011.

Whitesel. *Preparing for Change Reaction: How to Introduce Change in Your Church.* Indianapolis: Wesleyan Publishing House, 2007.

Practical Tools for Reinventing the Dying Church

Whitesel, Bob and Kent R. Hunter. *A House Divided: Bridging the Generation Gaps in Your Church*. Nashville: Abingdon Press, 2000.

Winseman, Albert L. *Growing an Engaged Church: How to Stop Doing Church and Start Being the Church Again*. New York: Gallup Press, 2009.

Wood, Gene. *Leading Turnaround Churches*. St. Charles, IL: ChurchSmart Resources, 2001.

Wood, Gene and Daniel Harkavy. *Leading Turnaround Teams*. St. Charles, IL: ChurchSmart Resources, 2004.

Wood, George O. "Eight Principles to Revitalizing Your Church" http:enrichmentjournal.ag.org/201001_024_8_principles.cfm (assessed October 10, 2010).

Wood, Leon J. *Distressing Days of the Judges*, Grand Rapids: Zondervan, 1975.

Wood, Richard E. Survival of Rural America: Small Victories and Better Harvests. Lawrence, KA: University Press of Kansas, 2008.

Yonkman, Todd Grant. Reconstructing Church: Tools for Turning Your Congregation Around. Lanham, Maryland: Rowman & Littlefield, 2014

Youmans, Peter. "My Church's Inferiority Complex," *Leadership a Practical Journal for Church Leaders* Volume XXIV (Fall 2003): 78-81.

Practical Tools for Reinventing the Dying Church

ABOUT THE GENERAL EDITOR

Dr. Tom Cheyney
Founder & Directional Leader
Renovate National Church Revitalization Conference
RenovateConference.org
ChurchRevitalizer.guru
tom@renovateconference.org

Tom is the founder and directional leader of the RENOVATE National Church Revitalization Conference, Executive Editor of *the Church Revitalizer Magazine*, and leader of the RENOVATE Church Revitalization Bootcamps where he mentors pastors, churches, and denominational leaders in Church Revitalization and Renewal all across North America. He serves as the National Host of the weekly Church Revitalization and Renewal Podcast.

Dr. Cheyney has written over 5,000 print, audio resources, guides, and books for Church Revitalizers, pastors, church planters, and lay leaders. His most recent books include: *The Seven Pillars of Church Revitalization and Renewal: The Biblical Foundation for Revitalization, The Church Revitalizer as Change Agent, The Nuts and Bolts of church Revitalization (*along with Terry Tials*); Thirty Eight Church Revitalization Models for the Twenty First Century* and *Preaching Towards Church Revitalization and Renewal (*along with Larry Wynn*)*. Cheyney has also written along with his friend Rodney Harrison *Spin-Off Churches* (B&H Publishers). Tom is a nationally recognized conference speaker and a frequent writer on church revitalization, church planting, new church health, and leadership development. Others have labeled Tom as the *Father of the Church Revitalization Movement* as his influence has stretched across multiple denominations and countries.

The Renovate Group is passionate about helping hurting and dying churches break out of the ruts of decline and get growing again. The group's primary goal is to see the renewing of the monumental number of churches that have done little to turn around the decline and now have few options remaining to them.

Tom Cheyney